TENZIN GYATSO

TENZIN GYATSO

THE EARLY LIFE
OF THE DALAI LAMA

CLAUDE B. LEVENSON

translated from the French by
Joseph Rowe

NORTH ATLANTIC BOOKS
BERKELEY, CALIFORNIA

Published by
North Atlantic Books
P.O. Box 12327
Berkeley, California 94712

Printed in the United States of America
Cover and book design © Ayelet Maida, A/M Studios
Cover and text photographs courtesy Tibetan archives; author photograph on page 155 © Jean-Claude Buhrer-Solal

Tenzin Gyatso: The Early Life of the Dalai Lama is sponsored by the Society for the Study of Native Arts and Sciences, a nonprofit educational corporation whose goals are to develop an educational and crosscultural perspective linking various scientific, social, and artistic fields; to nurture a holistic view of arts, sciences, humanities, and healing; and to publish and distribute literature on the relationship of mind, body, and nature.

North Atlantic Books' publications are available through most bookstores. For further information, call 800-337-2665 or visit our website at www.northatlanticbooks.com.

Substantial discounts on bulk quantities are available to corporations, professional associations, and other organizations. For details and discount information, contact our special sales department.

Library of Congress Cataloging-in-Publication Data
Levenson, Claude B.
  [Dalai-Lama. English]
  Tenzin Gyatso : the Dalai Lama from birth to exile / by Claude B. Levenson ; translated by Joseph Rowe.
     p. cm.
  ISBN 1-55643-383-2 (pbk.)
  1. Bstan-(r)'zin-rgya-mtsho, Dalai Lama xiv, 1935–   2. Dalai lamas—Biography.   3. Tibet (China)—Politics and government—1951–   I. Rowe, Joseph, 1942–   II. Title.

BQ7935.B777 T3613 2001
294.3'63 dc21
[B]
                                                        2001054371

1 2 3 4 5 6 7 8 9 / 06 05 04 03 02

You have your own path
and there is no one ahead to show you the way.

Each person creates reality
and must take responsibility for it.

         –Gautama Buddha

Contents

Author's Introduction
to the First American Edition

It is with great pleasure that I have learned that this book will now be accessible to the English-speaking world for the first time, due to the good offices of Richard Grossinger at North Atlantic Books, and the skilled translation work of Joseph Rowe. I wish to take this opportunity to thank them.

I realize that the Dalai Lama is a famous figure in America, and that there are already a number of good books in English about him, most of which I am familiar with. But my original motivation in writing this book remains in the feeling that insufficient attention has been given to his life before exile—especially to its social and political aspects—and to what this period reveals when placed in a wider context. Perhaps this could help us to better understand why he has become what he is. In my view, the multiple facets of his rich and extraordinary personality are of course expressions of his unique being, acting spontaneously in the present moment; but they have also been equally fashioned by past circumstances, the influence of his intimates, his mentors, his spiritual teachers, and by the immense landscapes and traditions of his native country itself. What emerges from all this is a man of unmistakable inner power, in whom an unshakable faith and positive attitude have taken root: a gift which is freely given, available to all who come in contact with him.

It was by lucky accident (though in Buddhism there are no accidents) that I was able to become friends with the Dalai Lama, during a period when his fame was much less widespread than it is now. This ultimately led to many long conversations, and to a personal relationship which stands out like a bright red thread in the tapestry of my journalistic career. In the early 1980s I learned much about the occupation of his country, the loyalty of his people in spite of the repression, and the ravages of an insane policy whose goal is annihilation, and which has already resulted in irreparable damage. These discoveries were the initial basis of a long series of dialogues which finally grew into the first French-language biography of the fourteenth Dalai Lama, *Le Seigneur du lotus blanc (Lord of the White Lotus),* published in Paris in 1987, with later editions in English, German, Danish, Spanish, and Romanian. A number of passages from that book are quoted in the present work.

Over the years I have made a number of visits to the Dalai Lama's current residence in Dharamsala. But other cities in India—Bodh Gaya, Darjeeling, Sarnath, Bungler, and Delhi—have also been places of highly informative meetings, especially with his sister, Jetsun Pema, who directs the network of Tibetan children's villages. These are devoted to helping the youngest exiles preserve the essence of their heritage, whose survival is now threatened both inside and outside Tibet. I have also spent many hours speaking with refugees, both recent and from the earliest days. Though quite diverse, all of these interviews bear similar witness to the clear and obstinate will of an entire people not to allow themselves to be obliterated by the world's indifference and complicity in the Chinese campaign of destruction of their country. Several voyages there have allowed me to see for myself the continuing deterioration of the situation, and to verify that Tibet is in serious danger of becoming engulfed and reduced to a mere Chinese province, a place where Tibetans are finally ground down to the status of a powerless and marginal people in their own land.

Turning mainly to my profession as writer to help in this situation, I first published *Le chemin de Lhassa (The Road from Lhassa)* in 1985, which told of my initial encounter with the stark reality of

Tibet under the Chinese yoke. A number of articles and other books followed. This was the period before the watershed of the Nobel Peace Prize in 1989, when ignorance and indifference to the suffering of the Tibetans were much more prevalent than now.

In another vein, I published several long interviews with the Dalai Lama dealing more with the subject of his teachings. I also translated others from English, including two books of conversations with scientists: *Sleeping, Dreaming, Dying,* by Francisco Varela, and *Gentle Bridges,* by Hayward and Varela.

I also chose to become an active member of various groups of support for Tibet in France, Italy, Switzerland, Belgium, and Mexico. Since its foundation in 1992, I have had the honor of belonging to the Committee of 100 for Tibet. This group has made a tremendous effort to make the voice of Tibetans heard wherever necessary, so that justice may finally have a chance to be granted to them. The worth of their civilization and of their very lives has been too long ignored in the name of "realistic politics" at the highest levels of government and international bodies, by those who claim to be world leaders.

May the present book be read with this perspective in mind, and bring insight to the reader. As the Dalai Lama never tires of repeating: "Tolerance, patience, and courage are signs not of defeat, but of victory."

Claude B. Levenson
June, 2001

Over the Himalayas to Freedom

In mid April, 1959, a great celebration took place at the Tawang monastery. Perched at almost ten thousand feet, overlooking the valley of Arunachal Pradesh on the Indian side of the Himalayan slopes, the place was so remote that time seemed suspended. The dancer lamas were dressed in their most lavish costumes, giant drums and horns had blasted resounding peals to all the horizons, and the walls of the vast stone hall rustled and echoed with the movements of sacred dance and prayer.

The Dalai Lama had returned. After centuries since his last visit, and under extremely arduous circumstances, the supreme dignitary of Tibetan Buddhism had finally kept his promise to return, thereby fulfilling a prophecy handed down through so many generations that it had now been forgotten by most.

Ever since 1689 C.E., a memory had lived on in this distant and lonely retreat where several hundred monks lived together, sharing daily work, prayer, and contemplation. It was the memory of a most remarkable visitor: a child of six from the nearby village, who had been brought to the monastery before setting out on the long road to Lhassa. Accompanied by his regent, he had just been discovered and recognized by the latter as the sixth reincarnation of the Dalai Lama. The child was just setting out on his way to take on this destiny under the new name of Tsangyang Gyatso (Ocean of Melody). This young man would also turn out to be a poet and rebel whose behavior was so different from that expected of a priest-king that it caused him grave problems, ultimately costing him his throne.

That child had been visibly reluctant to leave his native hamlet of Urgeling, near the Tawang monastery. It is said that he stood for some time before a sapling in front of the monastery, and declared: "When the three limbs of this tree have grown to equal height, I shall return." A scribe had noted the words of the prescient child, and preserved them on parchment protected by a richly embroidered cover which was kept in a special corner of the monastery library, gathering the dust of centuries along with other relics containing prophecies and spells.

This prophecy would only be fulfilled well into the second half of the tormented twentieth century, shortly after the pivotal crisis in Lhassa in March, 1959. By this time a few lamas were well aware that the small tree had grown into a large and strong one, and that three of its main limbs had indeed attained the same height, covered by rich and flourishing leaves. These lamas were among the few who were not astonished when it was suddenly learned that the Dalai Lama would be passing discreetly through Tawang, headed for the border and for exile.

This twenty-four-year-old man whom the monks welcomed with grandest honors was vastly different from the child who had left the village three centuries ago. Besides the difference in chronological age, and the several lifetimes which separated him from his predecessor, Tenzin Gyatso had just been through a month of travel under severe hardships. Their caravan had encountered torrential rainstorms, sandstorms, and blizzards, as well as dangerous mudslides, icy trails, and blinding sunlight at critical mountain passes. It was as if nature herself were unleashing hostile forces to amplify the bitterness of his new road of exile. Under the protection of Khampa warriors, the caravan wound its slow but inexorable way through village, hamlet, fortress, and monastery, surrounded by an atmosphere of dramatic flight through danger, and often by the aura of a mythic tale.

On the road to exile.

Their voyage had taken them on one of the most dangerous and comfortless horseback rides on the planet, through a series of passes over nineteen thousand feet high. Traveling for about ten hours a day, the exhausted humans and animals had to deal with severe weather and very scanty rations of food and provisions, as well as with obstructions from landslides, which necessitated frequent dismounting. The older members of the party, as well as those overly accustomed to the comforts of city life, struggled just to survive. Yet all of them realized that the caravan had to push on regardless of the cost, for it was virtually certain that they were being pursued by the Chinese.

On the other hand, there were unexpected blessings and moments of great happiness—for example, that desolate mountain pass shrouded in fog, where a farmer mysteriously appeared out of nowhere with the gift of a white horse for the Dalai Lama, and then disappeared back into the mists. And there was the time at Lhuntse Dzong, shortly after a secret courier had arrived on horseback to inform them that Peking had just dissolved the Tibetan government. The caravan halted right there, and ritual ceremonies were performed to proclaim the official formation of a new provisional Tibetan government. Even though this act by the Dalai Lama had no apparent political power, it was an important demonstration of his determination to oppose the Chinese destruction of Tibetan institutions and culture.

Other bits of news which came to them were just as grim: Lhassa had been bombarded, thousands of Tibetans had been massacred, and fear and violence had multiplied when the foreign military authorities learned of the Dalai Lama's absence.

The last part of their voyage was probably the most painful, as well as the most frightening. Barely had they crossed the Karpo pass when a biplane appeared, flying low over the long line of the struggling caravan. No one knew for certain what it was, but it was almost certainly a Chinese airplane, and a sign that the caravan had been spotted. However, nothing came of this, and two days later they reached Mangmang, the last Tibetan hamlet before the border. From there, the winds of freedom could be felt from the Indian village of Chhuthangmo not far away.

Yet a final trial was in store for the Dalai Lama before he would reach Tawang and then leave his country for good. A torrential rain fell that night, thoroughly drenching all the tents. Early the next morning, Tenzin Gyatso woke up very ill, too weak to travel further. A radio news bulletin from India later reported that he had been seriously wounded by a fall from his horse—he wryly commented that at least he had been spared that misfortune—but he had to spend the whole day resting in a hut under wretched conditions. His health was not getting any better, but it was decided that they could not risk waiting longer, and he left the following day with his closest companions. Too weak to ride a horse, he was strapped onto the back of a *dzo,* a cross between a yak and a cow. It was this placid and imperturbable animal which bore him down the slopes toward a new phase of his life.

He badly needed the rest and hospitality lavished upon him at the Tawang monastery. People arrived by the hundreds from neighboring farms and villages to pay homage to the Dalai Lama, and this fervent devotion was like a balm to his heart. But he could not stay long at Tawang, and three days later they set off again on their voyage into the unknown. They were confident of reaching India now, but they did not know that it was an India which was to be a land of seemingly permanent exile. This would not only entail new responsibilities to those he had left behind, it would also thrust him into a new international prominence and a political role which he did not find easy to play.

In spite of this apparent victory of the Chinese, it is said that Mao Tse-tung himself, upon learning of the Dalai Lama's safe arrival in India, somberly commented: "We have lost the battle for Tibet."

From Tawang to Bomdila, the caravan, now protected by a company of Assam Rifles, continued on its way without incident. They crossed through the last pine forests, which gave way into the Dirang valley, filled with wild orchids. From now on it was to their rear that the vast chain of the Himalayas would bar the way. The last phase took them down into the warm mists of the Ganges plain. Their last stop in relative calm and tranquility was at Khylong. After that they began to encounter the crowds gathered at Tezpur, which included devotees, curiosity seekers, and journalists. Tawang was a little over a hundred miles, and several days' travel, behind them.

At Tezpur there was a special reception awaiting him, as well as hundreds of telegrams of sympathy. Upon his arrival he issued a statement which was both measured and brief, expressing his sorrow for the tragedy taking place in Tibet, and his gratitude for his welcome in India. In cautious terms, he described what he had just been through, and his hope that the bloodshed would stop. From this time on, and entirely apart from the special traditional veneration of him, the Dalai Lama was to stand as a living symbol of the survival of Tibetan culture, and a torch-bearer of hope for his own people.

Now, forty years later, with Tibet itself occupied, dismembered, and subjected to brutal expropriation on all levels, Tenzin Gyatso, the fourteenth of his lineage, has paradoxically become the most present and the most popular of all his predecessors.

I Leave for Lhassa

My very earliest memories... Surely they resemble those of many other people, and I've never attached any special importance to them. I loved to follow my mother when she went to get eggs from the chicken coop. I would stay there and amuse myself with the chickens, it was so nice and warm in the straw. The house where I was born in the village of Taktser was filled with a loving family atmosphere, though our conditions of life were humble, like all farmers then.

I also have a very clear memory of a fight among some children, when I leaped to the defense of the weaker ones. My two oldest brothers had already left for their studies—the eldest to the Kumbum monastery, and the other to the village school nearby. Lobsang Samten was still at home, before being sent in his turn to Kumbum. In those days my sister Tsering Dolma helped my mother take care of me—she was the eldest child, eighteen years older than I.

As for signs and presages, I really don't know. There are things that I remember, but also things that others have told me. Perhaps some of these could be interpreted as signs, but sometimes it's only long afterwards that one understands them in that way. Thus it is said that I always wanted to be seated at the place of honor at the family table, and that only my mother had the right to touch my bowl. I'm also told that I would often pack up some belongings in a cloth and bundle them on a stick, saying that I was leaving for Lhassa. Tsering Dolma, who often helped my mother, told me several times that I was born with my eyes wide open. Also, it is said that I was never frightened by passing strangers, and that I enjoyed their company. And I apparently didn't like for others to contradict me. . . .

I have later memories of being slapped soundly, once by my father for pulling on his mustache, and another time by his brother for scattering the pages of a sacred text from which he said his evening prayers. . . . And I also remember one of my brothers being smacked. But that was after I had been recognized as the incarnation of the Dalai Lama, after which no one dared raise a hand against me any more. Even my masters who taught me at the Potala did not strike me—in the study room there were two whips, one for my brother, who shared my studies for a time, and the other for me. His was made of leather, whereas mine was made of silk. Most of the time, the masters had only to make a motion of reaching for a whip. But Lobsang Samten was not always as fortunate as I. . . . On the whole, there's nothing so remarkable about all this, is there?[1]

Perhaps there isn't. And yet. . .

The fourteenth Dalai Lama ponders his early childhood memories with detachment, punctuated at times with an expressive laugh, and with no trace of nostalgia or regret. These are memories, nothing more, like those of any other person's life. . .

And yet from the moment that little Lhamo Thondup was formally recognized as the reincarnation and successor of the thirteenth Dalai Lama, a new life began for him. It was not yet radically different from that of other special Tibetan children who were chosen to be sent to monasteries. But already a destiny far from the ordinary had begun to express itself.

The turning point was the arrival of a small ecclesiastical group of travelers in the village of Taktser, asking for hospitality at the family house. As is the custom in Tibet, this was unquestioningly

---

[1] From a personal conversation with the author.

granted, and considered an honor and blessing for the family. The dignitaries were lodged in the best room at the north of the house, and the servants in the kitchen areas, near the porch at the entry. The highest-ranking lama, Kewtsang Rinpoche, had disguised himself as a servant. This gave him the opportunity to investigate the surroundings without attracting the family's attention, in an attempt to verify certain signs which had been previously furnished by oracles and masters.

These envoys from Lhassa had spent several weeks on the road before arriving at the great monastery of Kumbum. They had been guided there by a reflection seen on the surface of the sacred lake of Lhamo Latso. Several high lamas had gone to the lake in formal procession in order to search for signs. In its waters, they had clearly recognized the peculiarities of the statuary and roof decorations of three-storied Kumbum. This vision was a confirmation that they were on the right track in their search for the new Dalai Lama.

They made use of their brief stay there to meet with local lamas and learn of any rumors or news in the surrounding country which might aid their search. Although the arrival of such a party from Lhassa obviously implied a special mission, it was not suspected how special it was, because such missions were not that rare in Tibet.

Thus the subterfuge chosen by Kewtsang Rinpoche would help him to get some impressions about the personality of this farmer's son without arousing expectations which might bias the information. They had already heard that he was very intelligent, and that he sometimes surprised those around him by his precocious remarks. At almost ten thousand feet, the hamlet of Taktser comprised about a dozen households. Like other similar communities scattered about in the immensity of the Tibetan plateau, it also served as a resting place for infrequent voyagers passing that way. The older brother of the Dalai Lama recalls:

My family was poor in those days, as was the whole village. However, we all had beautiful costumes for special occasions, and these were kept in the best room of the house, carefully laid out in huge wooden chests.

Such flat-roofed houses are typically found in the fields, sometimes grouped around an interior courtyard, with the whole compound surrounded by a protective wall of adobe bricks.

The main courtyard was often the domain of alert watchmen who guarded the herds there during the night. They also protected the farmers' houses from any brigands who might try to attack. Free at night, these fierce and powerful men were kept in chains during the day, supposedly because of their terrible reputation—but also in order to impress and dissuade any potential robbers who might pass by.

The hills around Taktser were lush with wild berries, which the children went to pick in season, so as to supplement a diet which was rather meager most of the time. The generally modest agricultural plots were distributed among the villagers. These provided a subsistence diet based on barley, with cows and *dri* (the female yak) providing milk, dried cheese, and butter. When allowed to turn slightly rancid, yak butter is an indispensable ingredient of the famous Tibetan butter tea, a thick and robust beverage whose strong flavor is especially loved by nomads.

Traveling merchants and traders also provided various necessary goods to villages at more or less regular intervals. Artisans such as tailors and cobblers also followed a traditional itinerary, stopping to offer their services and renovate modest village wardrobes according to the need of the moment. Some ten miles from the village, a small monastery served as a religious center, and its monks occasionally visited homes to recite prayers or perform ceremonies required by various events. Also, a house would always have a domestic altar for daily worship, typically located in the most beautiful and spacious room. A butter lamp always burned there, and there were representations of the family's protective divinities.

When the high lama arrived in Taktser disguised as a servant, he knew that he was on the right track. From the road, he could already see the turquoise-colored tiles and gutters made of juniper wood. These unusual features had been noted on the house seen in the vision on the waters of the sacred lake. And in the courtyard there was a brown and black spotted dog, just as in the strange vision which had previously been written down by scribes. It remained to find the child, and examine him to be sure that he met the precise requirements.

Like the other villagers, the family of the future Dalai Lama eked out a living from the hard work on the father's plot of land, and from their three or four cows which grazed along with the others in the village herd. They had suffered stoically through hardships in recent years: an unexpected drought that hurt crops, as well as an animal that died, and another that disappeared. In Tibetan tradition, it is said that the birth of such an exceptional child always comes with a price to the family. Sometimes the cost is high, though this is often appreciated only long after the event. Again, the older brother of the Dalai Lama remembers:

> The simple life we led at Taktser was technically one of poverty, but was never lacking in warmth and comfort. There was always at least enough to eat, and on holidays my mother would always find some way to cook some special treats for us, and for any visitors who might happen to be there. [...] Never for an instant would we have considered ourselves as poor. We were just aware of being happy, both as family members and as villagers.[2]

---

[2] Thubten Jigme Norbu and Colin Turnbull, *Tibet, its History, Religion and People* (New York: Penguin, 1969).

While the supposedly important visitors exchanged courtesies and conversation with the mistress of the house over a bowl of tea, the really important visitor was in the kitchen, sitting in front of the hearth. A lively child climbed boldly over his knees, and made a strenuous effort to grab a rosary hanging on the disguised lama's neck. He imperiously ordered the monk to "Give it back!" Joining in the game, the monk agreed to give it to him, but only on condition that the boy tell him who he was. The reply was immediate: "I'm a lama from Sera, and that is my rosary!" In fact, this rosary had belonged to the thirteenth Dalai Lama. Kewtsang Rinpoche gave it to the child without flinching, but without saying anything. Although this display had virtually convinced him personally, he still had to confirm it with further evidence, and also to report everything to his superiors. Another surprising thing about the child was that he had just spoken in the elegant dialect of Lhassa, which was practically unknown in the remote area of Taktser.

Very early the next morning, as the visitors prepared to take their leave, the monks were astonished to see little Lhamo Thondup appear with a bundle on a stick, ready to go with them. Rather confused, his mother came and ordered him back in the house, but he began to cry, stamping his feet and imperiously proclaiming that "my people" had come there in order to "take me back to my big monastery." Kewtang Rinpoche had to intervene, tenderly assuring the child that it was not yet time, and that he promised to return. Only this promise calmed the child. Of this particular episode, the only thing the Dalai Lama himself now remembers is the eagle-eye of one of the lamas upon him. This was Sherab Tenzin, who was to become one of his three closest personal servants, and who taught him the rudiments of writing.

The messengers did indeed return some days later, this time as official examiners. Yet they still did not reveal the full identity of the *tulku*[3] who was the object of their search. Their avowed mission was

---

[3] *Tulku* is the general term for the reincarnated essence of a deceased master or sage.

to submit the boy to an "examination of prior memories." This consisted essentially of having him recognize an object which had been important to him, by having him choose it from among an assortment of other objects, many of which were quite rich and attractive in appearance. The examiners accorded special importance to this process, especially when it involved finding the authentic successor of a high wisdom-lineage, and above all when they were searching for the reincarnation of the Dalai Lama or the Panchen Lama, the two most important figures in the hierarchy of Tibetan Buddhism.

This was not the first time the family had experienced such a moment. The eldest boy, Thubten Jigme Norbu, had been tested in a similar way before being taken to the neighboring monastery of Taktser, where he lived for awhile before taking formal vows at Kumbum monastery. He was studying there when his younger brother was discovered in his own turn. Nevertheless, it is rare for more than one *tulku* to appear in the same family, and no one yet suspected that this might be the Dalai Lama himself.

Some years later, however, there were some villagers who recalled that back in 1909, the thirteenth Dalai Lama had passed through the area while returning from a voyage to Mongolia. He had been very pleased by his sojourn in a nearby hermitage called Karma Shartsong, and several times had expressed his admiration for the beauty of the surrounding country. Before leaving the area, he had left behind a pair of boots. For Tibetans, this was a sure sign that he would return. Some even claim that he stared long on several occasions at the farm where his successor was to be born twenty-four years later.

According to all eyewitnesses, the three-year-old Lhamo Thondup was quite undaunted by the examination. After having first satisfied themselves that the body of the child had the thirty-two secret major and minor marks which are supposed to be signs of a spiritual heritage, the emissaries from Lhassa randomly spread a number of objects on a low table: rosaries, canes, several *damaru*[4] drums, more or less precious bowls, and several other items for daily use, both religious and ordinary.

With practically no hesitation, the child chose his objects with confidence, unfazed by the keen and unwavering regards of the venerable visitors. It was without a single mistake. There was only one moment of hesitation in which it seemed he might make an error— after picking up a well-used cane, he examined it closely and then changed his mind, exchanging it for another one which was known by the examiners to have belonged to the thirteenth Dalai Lama. Yet this particular hesitation only reinforced the examiners' certainty of the identity of the child, for it turned out that the first cane he had selected had in fact originally belonged to the previous Dalai Lama, but that he had long ago made a present of it to one of his faithful servants. Another significant event was when the boy picked up an obviously well-used *damaru*,[4] and began to play it resoundingly, with a natural ease that astonished the old monks.

Although they felt certain of the identity of the *tulku,* the emissaries from Lhassa nevertheless followed the caution required by tradition, and left again to inform the religious and governmental authorities of these results. Several more weeks were to elapse before these would be confirmed, and life at the family farm at Taktser quickly returned to its usual calm. Yet there remained a sense of amazement in the air, and now people began to find explanations for certain unusual phenomena of recent years—the unseasonable hailstorms which had damaged the harvest, sudden strange and destructive storms, and inexplicable illnesses. It also made more sense now that the boy's father had been strangely bedridden during most of the months of his wife's pregnancy, without any physician or lama being able to find an explanation for it. This strange illncss vanished as mysteriously as it had come with the birth of his

---

[4] *Damaru* is a drum used in tantric rituals. It has an hourglass form like that of the traditional drum of Shiva, with two resonant heads struck by balls which swing on cords.

son. That very day he arose from his bed fresh and full of energy, going immediately to work in the fields as if nothing had happened.

His mother remembered the pregnancy as a painful one, with a surprising dream on the night before his birth: two blue dragons came to bow low to her, with great pomp and ceremony.

Of these weeks of waiting for the return of the emissaries from Lhassa, the Dalai Lama especially remembers a pair of crows who began to perch regularly on a corner of their roof. To Tibetans, such an image recalls the story of the first Dalai Lama, who was protected from brigands by a crow when only a baby, hidden by his mother in the hollow of a rock. In all succeeding incarnations of the lineage, there would appear to be a special relationship with crows. The jet-black plumage of this bird symbolizes the formidable deity Mahakala, the Black Lord of transcendental wisdom, also known as the personification of Time.

In spite of the efforts of the masters from Lhassa to maintain discretion, news was beginning to spread about the new *tulku* who had been found in the village of Taktser. Rumors went so far as to suggest that it might indeed be the highest, the Dalai Lama himself. Unfortunately, these rumors reached the ears of a local Muslim warlord, Ma Pou-feng, who was allied with the Chinese, and whose reputation for violence was matched by that of his greed. He did not hesitate to demand a "right to depart" for the young *tulku,* for the enormous sum of one hundred thousand Chinese piasters—the equivalent of ninety thousand dollars today. While waiting for the ransom to be collected, Lhamo Thondup was brought to Kumbum monastery, where high lamas examined him further in order to be certain that he was indeed the one. In order to avoid a further raising of the ransom, as well as other obstacles, the envoys from Lhassa claimed that the examinations were not yet conclusive, and that the final decision would have to be made by the masters of the great monasteries of Lhassa.

Temporarily lodged in this monastic city, the child was surprised to be awakened very early one morning before dawn, and installed on a throne, amidst great ceremony. The hour had been chosen by astrologers. This was not yet the actual rite of entry into his monastic order, but was a semi-official preparatory rite. The atmosphere was sufficiently solemn to impress the child, and there were liturgical ceremonies which he had never seen—or had forgotten? The future sovereign of Tibet went through all this, reassured by the presence of his parents, who were deeply moved. But a short time later, they returned to Taktser, leaving their son in the care of the monks. The three-year-old boy must have felt lonely in the midst of this beehive of unfamiliar activity which was Kumbum in those days.

The monastery had been built in 1582, by command of the third Dalai Lama. Its location was the birthplace in 1357 of Tsong-Khapa, "the man of onion valley," a great scholar and reformer, and founder of the Gelug, one of the four great schools of Tibetan Buddhism.[5] The Gelugpa, also known as "the practitioners of virtue," and the "yellow hats," have become the school of the Dalai Lama. A major center of Tibetan wisdom and erudition, a veritable Buddhist university on the edge of the Chinese empire, Kumbum took its name from the "ten thousand images" of a miraculous tree, which local legend said had grown out of the hair of Tsong-Khapa, with leaves bearing sacred inscriptions on their undersides.

In any case, it was surely a long wait there for the three-year-old future Dalai Lama. He was treated with great consideration, but not that differently from other children of his age who were also waiting to begin their novitiate. Luckily, the old master who was put in charge of him was a man of great kindness, and allowed the child to wrap himself protectively in the folds of his capacious robes. One day, he offered the boy a peach, which was a very special treat. Lhamo Thondup also found a protective presence in Lobsang Samten, his older brother by three years, who was to become one

---

[5] The four major schools are: Nyingma, Kagyu, Sakya, and Gelug.

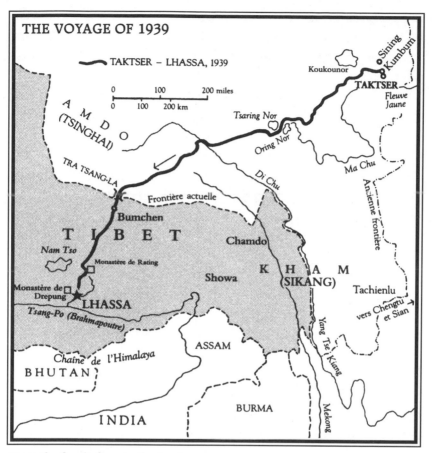

THE VOYAGE OF 1939

TAKTSER – LHASSA, 1939

0   100   200 miles
0   100   200 km

Sining
Kumbum
Koukounor
TAKTSER
Fleuve
Jaune

A M D O
(TSINGHAI)

Tsaring Nor
Oring Nor

Ma Chu

Ancienne frontière

TRA TSANG-LA

Di Chu

Frontière actuelle

Bumchen

T I B E T

Chamdo

Nam Tso

Monastère de Rating

Showa

K H A M
(SIKANG)

Monastère de
Drepung

Tachienlu

vers Chengtu
et Sian

LHASSA

Tsang-Po (Brahmapoutre)

Yang Tsé Kiang

Chaîne de l'Himalaya

ASSAM

BHUTAN

INDIA

BURMA

Mekong

From the family farm to the Potala.

Source: Tenzin Gyatso, fourteenth Dalai Lama, *Mon pays et mon peuple, Mémoires*
(Geneva: Olizane Publications, 1984).

of the closest companions in his life, sharing everything from studies and voyages to quarrels and mischievous stunts.

Yet his strongest memory of this period is one of solitude, and the sadness of a child separated from his family, feeling puzzled and abandoned. After all, what did it matter to the child whether he was, or was not, the Dalai Lama? In this experience, he unknowingly began an early initiation into human solitude itself. Such an initiation was perhaps more rigorous for any apprentice monk, especially one who was called to bear the burden of destiny for a whole people and country. But the child knew nothing of this consciously. Would he someday remember having chosen it?

The oldest of his brothers, Thubten Jigme Norbu, was himself the *tulku* of the chief lama of Taktser. He was sixteen at the time, too busy with his studies to spend much time with his younger brothers. In any case, custom decreed that they be raised by much older monks who would initiate them in the basics of monastic discipline. Very attached to his family, Thubten Jigme Norbu had difficulty persuading his masters to allow him to leave for Lhassa so as to pursue his training at Drepung, one of the three great *viharas*[6] of the capital. This was after his younger brother had moved there and officially assumed his destined role.

As the time of departure for Lhassa approached, with growing preparations, negotiations, and intrigues, Lhamo Thondup began to clearly perceive that he was at the center of all this complicated activity, and that his time was approaching. He especially understood that his long wait was now coming to an end, and he no longer languished for hours in a corner. He knew especially that he would soon see his mother again, of whom he was (and remained all his life) extremely fond.

All around him the monastery bustled with its typical activities, monks and novices busy at their tasks, seemingly without a care for the portentous events which were already being prepared. The

---

[6] *Vihara* is a Buddhist monastery.

ransom had been paid to Ma Pou-feng, but at the last moment the brigand suddenly changed his mind and demanded three times that sum.

Even here, the obstacle was removed as if by miracle: some Muslim merchants who were just leaving in a caravan for Mecca agreed to advance this sum, which would be promptly repaid to them when they passed through Lhassa. In mid-July of 1939, a week after his fourth birthday, the farmer's son from Taktser left Kumbum in a magnificent chariot, headed for the holiest city of Tibetan Buddhism. In Lhassa itself, great preparations were underway to welcome the arrival and homecoming of this newest emanation of Chenresig, or Avalokiteshvara, protective deity of Tibet, and *bodhisattva*[7] of infinite compassion.

The caravan from Kumbum to Lhassa took several weeks, and it must have made an impressive sight. Besides the Dalai Lama's brother, Lobsang Samten, and their parents, there were many religious dignitaries, including those who had examined him, as well as high government officials, trail guides, mule-drivers, merchants, and pilgrims. It was an extremely heterogeneous crowd, both secular and ecclesiastical, where people often had little idea of whom they were rubbing shoulders with. Nevertheless, all felt the momentousness of the situation, and were keenly aware of the priority to find a safe harbor for this precious young incarnation of the supreme religious and civil authority of their people.

In the *dreljam,* a sort of palanquin borne by mules, Lhamo Thondup and Lobsang Samten made themselves comfortable, chatting during pauses. The two children generally got along rather well, but the younger soon realized that his social status was higher than that of his elder, and he took shameless advantage of it. It got to the

---

[7] *Bodhisattva* is a fully awakened being of compassionate wisdom, who renounces the finality of nirvana, so as to help beings who are still caught up in the illusion of suffering. Chenresig is the Tibetan version of the Mahayana bodhisattva known in Sanskrit as Avalokiteshvara. The Dalai Lama tulku is considered to be an emanation of Avalokiteshvara.

point that any sort of remark from one or the other of them might set off a dispute, which typically became physical. The younger was sure of his status, and although the older was physically stronger, he had to exercise restraint due to the status of his younger brother. He was well aware of this, though the announcement had only been made public a few days after they had left Kumbum and the surrounding country where the tyrant Ma Pou-feng imposed his rule.

Once the news was out, the caravan took on an even more solemn air, partly because there were now rather rigid protocols and practices which had to be publicly observed. For the young Dalai Lama, this slow voyage was his first chance to see his country. Of course a four-year-old does not notice the same kind of things as an older person, and his attention was often captured by such sights as that of vast herds of wild yaks and kyangs, those legendary herbivores of the Tibetan plateau. His eyes also became accustomed to the passage of incredible herds of deer, whose flight was as rapid as a dream, along with flocks of wild geese who appeared and disappeared in the vast skies. Often this vast landscape was barren and deserted, punctuated here and there by monasteries standing proudly at the summit of a rocky promontory, or precariously perched on the flanks of a steep cliff wall. Far in the distance hamlets would appear every two or three days, so tiny that they seemed as if dropped there by accident, forgotten by time and human events.

And there were especially those unforgettable vast panoramas of immeasurable plains surrounded by gigantic, seemingly unscalable mountains. Even today, the Dalai Lama vividly remembers these mountainscapes as the most sumptuous and powerful on earth. And the power of this land seems to harbor and unleash natural forces to match. Sometimes the caravan would be slammed by storms of sand or dust, other times by snow and hail, and sometimes by winds so violent that yaks would lose their horns in them. There were also blinding reflections of light off of snow and ice, making progress very difficult.

It would seem that even one trip through such incomparable immensities, allowing one's eyes to roam endlessly along the snowy heights which surround them, must have a profound effect on a human being—perhaps offering a perspective which opens into vaster and more subtle dimensions of being and relationships. Today, this perspective both shapes and is reflected in the gaze of the Dalai Lama himself.

Having set out in midsummer, it was already autumn before the caravan caught its first glimpse of Lhassa in the distance. They had made various stops—in the rare towns along the way, sometimes in monasteries such as that of Reiting, where the regent had joined the convoy, or in hermitages such as that of Rekya. Not only had their path had to avoid various natural obstacles, they also were strictly enjoined to take into account certain astrological predictions, as well as those of the oracles. In those days such matters were taken very seriously indeed in the Land of Snows, where such signs played a vital role in the relationship between the natural elements and cultural and religious life.

At each camp, a somewhat festive atmosphere could be felt, a foretaste of the great festivities planned for the arrival of the chosen child in Lhassa. During years when Tibetans are deprived of "the Presence," as the incarnation of their sovereign and spiritual master is often known, they feel as orphans, disoriented by the absence of his recognized embodiment on earth. This profound organic link with the people as a whole, which has persisted in spite of all kinds of vicissitudes of history, is one of the strangest and most inexplicable aspects of the relationship of the Dalai Lama with his people and with those around him. Perhaps the best we can do is to simply note this phenomenon, before searching for a key to understanding it. In any case, different people will find different interpretations. As long ago as 1714, the Italian Jesuit traveler Ippolito Desideri claimed that:

> The Tibetans love the Dalai Lama because he has become a man thousands of times, taking on the tribulations and sufferings which afflict a fragile, decrepit, and mortal humanity.[8]

As the caravan approached the capital, it also began to swell with new fellow-travelers. Merchants, itinerant workers, devout monks, high lamas, and minor officials were among those who made up the great variety of this crowd of followers. They were united by a complex feeling in which the most ingenuous of faiths is mingled with an instinctive loyalty nourished by centuries of veneration.

A governmental delegation had been dispatched to meet the party, welcoming them in a ceremony held in a tent at dawn at Gashi Nakha. After the traditional three prostrations before the throne on which the child was sitting, the chief minister of the party bestowed a *khata*[9] scarf upon him, as well as presenting an official letter from the regent recognizing the authenticity of his rebirth. After the traditional offerings of tea and rice, there were precious gifts to be placed at the feet of the child, including ritual gold dishes, sacred texts, turquoise, and coral. He then climbed back into his gold-embroidered palanquin and was escorted to Nagchukha, and the small monastery of Shapten, known as the "Palace of True Peace." An atmosphere of deep joy pervaded everywhere, and both lamas and laity rejoiced together in the repeated chant: "A blessed sun now shines upon Tibet."

This celebration lasted for two entire days, during which the child delighted in all the chants and dances, both monastic and worldly, which amused him endlessly. There were also a number of short audiences where people came to ask his blessing. He gave it gracefully to all, as if he were already long accustomed to the role which he had not quite yet officially assumed.

---

[8] Filippo de Filippi, ed., *An Account of Tibet, the Travels of Ippolito Desideri of Pistoia* (London: Routledge & Sons Ltd., 1937); reprinted Delhi, 1995.

[9] *Khata* is a white shawl signifying good fortune, blessing, and welcome.

Slowed down by the crowd which pressed from all sides, the procession finally got on its way again, amidst the sounds of drums, trumpets, and ceremonial cymbals, and surrounded by the vivid colors of banners, prayer flags, and emblems. Slowly, it wound its way down the plain of Dogu-Thang, toward the gates of the holy city.

In the midst of a vast encampment especially set up for it, stood the Peacock Tent, stretched in yellow satin and reserved for the official governmental welcome of the new sovereign to the capital. A very artistic, richly-decorated throne had been specially made for the authentic incarnation of the fourteenth Dalai Lama on this solemn occasion. Next to the monastic tent stood other festival tents of blue and white colors, sheltering various officials and invited guests. From the most minor civil servants to the highest ministers, from abbots to high lamas of surrounding monasteries, there were representatives not only from all over Tibet, but from Nepal, Bhutan, India, China, and Great Britain, who had come to pay their respects, marking this new chapter in Tibetan history.

The Dalai Lama remembers the two days of this ceremony as a panorama involving the vastest numbers of people he had ever imagined possible in his brief new existence. And—he also confesses with a smile—a feeling of having come home again...

The child spent almost the whole of this time seated on the throne, fascinated with the spectacle in his honor continually unfolding all around him. He was intrigued by the presence of two white men there, one of them the blond-haired radio technician from the British embassy, and his supervisor, Hugh Richardson.

At one point some very old lamas were brought to him, and with both tenderness and rigor, had him answer some very precise questions. Their conclusion was without reserve: it is he indeed. Several other witnesses to this occasion were struck by the confidence of the child, who also showed a remarkable friendliness which surprised almost all who approached him. Already people were speaking of such things as the "extraordinary acuity of his regard, a patience very rare for a child of that age, and a seemingly innate mastery of ritual gestures, as well as the beauty of his hands," as the British representative wrote.

Finally the entry into the city of Lhassa itself took place on the twenty-fifth day of the eighth month of the year of the Earth Rabbit, 2066. This translates to October 8, 1939, C.E. The procession wound through the city surrounded by a crowd in which reverence and joy were joined as one. Suddenly the Nechung oracle appeared: a man in deep trance, who jumped onto the Dalai Lama's palanquin, and pulled back the curtain, jerkily throwing a handful of rice upon the child. After this benediction he prostrated, and offered the white *khata* shawl. The contorted face of the medium, dressed in all his strange ritual trappings, is said to have so frightened the horses that they had to be restrained. Yet the child lama greeted him with serenity like an old friend, and also placed a *khata* shawl around his own neck in return.

The first stop was at Jokhang, the holiest sanctuary of Tibetan Buddhism, wherein the most venerated and precious statue of Tibet, the Jowo Shakyamuni Buddha, has been enthroned since the eighth century, C.E. The ceremony of thanksgiving and allegiance completed, trumpets and ritual conch shells began to sound, and the caravan now proceeded to the summer palace, known as Norbulingka, the "Park of Jewels," where the Dalai Lama and his entourage were to be lodged for a time. Whatever might happen in the rest of the world writhing in its torments beyond the vast reaches of the Himalayas, this world was now at peace. The only thing that mattered in this landscape of the gods was that the Protector of Tibet had just returned home.

From One Incarnation to Another

From a Buddhist perspective, the passage from life to death and back to life again is the most normal of occurrences, within the vast cycle of *samsara*,[10] which can only be escaped through Awakening. This is, or should be, the goal of all human existence. Reincarnation is a cornerstone of the Buddhist worldview. For Tibetan Buddhists, there is not the slightest doubt of a real continuity between the life of the current Dalai Lama and those of his predecessors. His biography is the latest chapter in a story which began in the fifteenth century, C.E., and which has profoundly influenced the events which make up the singular history of the Land of Snows.

According to the fourteenth Dalai Lama, "There are different levels of consciousness for Buddhist practitioners. When we are dealing with the deepest such level, which we call the subtle mind, it is entirely possible for this consciousness to be independent of brain and body. This subtle mind might perhaps be linked to the notion of reincarnation, and could shed light on what are sometimes called memories of previous lives."[11]

Yet he also shows much caution and reserve in discussing this subject, which is so full of pitfalls and confusion. As far as his own case is concerned, he has often pointed out that the office of Dalai Lama is a human institution, and as such is subject to the same

---

[10] *Samsara* (Sanskrit) is the endless cycle of deaths and rebirths seen in its illusory and unconscious aspect, both as events within one physical lifetime and over many such lifetimes. Literally, "going around in circles."

[11] Claude B. Levenson, *Le Seigneur du Lotus blanc* (Paris: Livre de Poche, 1989).

impermanence as other such institutions. Some day it will no doubt disappear. Might he in fact be the last of his lineage, as a persistent rumor keeps saying?

"It is up to the Tibetan people to decide this. If the institution has run its course, it is useless to try to prolong it. Historically, Tibet existed long before there was any Dalai Lama, and can surely survive quite well without one. As for myself personally, I am first and foremost just a monk, a simple Buddhist monk. In this sense I do have something to accomplish, a task which is perhaps directly linked with Tibet."[12]

In fact, the system of transmission of traditional wisdom through reincarnational lineages of masters first appeared in Tibet in the twelfth century, as part of the confluence of ancient beliefs coming from India. It first took root in the heart of the school known as the Karmapa lineage of masters. These reincarnated adepts would assure that the teachings passed from generation to generation would remain both unadulterated and relevant to the new times. Such is the theory, which of course assumes that this ancient knowledge corresponds to a fundamental existential reality, which is able to adapt itself according to the times and places in which it is newly formulated.

It was much later that the Dalai Lama lineage appeared, and came to dominate Tibetan history with the Tsong-Khapa reform, which took place at that pivotal moment between the fourteenth and fifteenth centuries, when the Gelugpa school was founded. It was an essentially religious lineage in the beginning, but slowly grew into a governmental structure as well, responding to the evolution of Tibetan society. This amplification culminated in the fifth Dalai Lama, who became the foremost spiritual and temporal power of the High Country.

The title of "Dalai Lama" itself did not appear until still later, in 1578. It is attributed to Altan Khan, a Mongol successor of Kublai

---

[12] Claude B. Levenson, *Le Seigneur du Lotus blanc,* (Paris: Livre de Poche, 1989).

Khan, as a title conferred by him on his spiritual teacher, Sonam Gyatso, a Tibetan lama of great wisdom and erudition. The words come from Mongolian *talé* (*Dalai* in Tibetan), meaning "ocean," and "lama" as the traditional title which attributes wisdom. Hence the title might be translated as "ocean of wisdom." However, the Tibetans themselves consider the institution as beginning in the fifteenth century with Gedun Truppa. It has continued unbroken to our day, in spite of the misfortunes which have befallen certain holders of the lineage.

A son of humble nomadic herdsmen from the central Tibetan high plateaus, Gedun Truppa showed a lively interest for study and religion at an early age. When he was seven his father died, and he was placed in a monastery in service to a monk, studying informally, and encountered the master Tsong-Khapa when he was twenty years old. He began to study assiduously with the latter, completing his tantric courses with one of the master's closest disciples. He later built the famous Tashilhumpo monastery at Shigatse, following the example of the foundation of Ganden by Tsong-Khapa, and the construction of Drepung at the edge of Lhassa. On his deathbed, he enjoined his disciples to "remember the teachings of the Lord Buddha and meditate upon them with utmost religious passion."

Because of the strict celibacy which had been re-established in the Gelug school by Tsong-Khapa, a different way had to be found for passing on lineages of masters. Since the *tulku* notion was already a familiar one by now in Tibet, an ever greater emphasis began to be placed on these *tulkus*, supposed to be repositories of knowledge from other lives, since traditional belief had long held that great sages and ascetics had the power to choose their next incarnation. Hence it was announced that the deceased master had returned in the body of an especially gifted young monk, Gedun Gyatso.

Becoming well-established after this, the institution was to go through its high and low points in the following centuries, right down to the present time. The traditional isolation and secrecy associated with Tibet have created all sorts of legends concerning this central personage, who has also become inseparably linked with the image of that country.

The Panchen Lama also plays an important role in his own right, especially regarding his reputation of erudition, but his function has been strictly limited to a spiritual one. Sometimes the vicissitudes of history have pushed this second-highest dignitary of Tibetan Buddhism into the limelight, especially in the twentieth century. Yet this has never led to any modification of foreign powers' recognition of the Dalai Lama as the primary dignitary. Relations between the two have sometimes been complicated by intrigues among the entourages of various high lamas, leading to a certain mistrust between the two groups which has been difficult to dissipate.

In parallel with religious developments, social and political history have had their own effects on matters. The growth in power of the Mongol empire brought about a concession by the royal family in favor of the fourth Dalai Lama, who was none other than the grandson of Altan Khan. Yongten Gyatso reigned for barely fifteen years. Yet this was enough to consolidate the links between Tibet and Mongolia, preparing the way for the arrival of a most important personage in Tibetan history, Ngawang Lobsang Gyatso, the fifth Dalai Lama.

Born in 1617, this child was taken at the age of five to Drepung monastery to be trained in his role. While he was perfecting his religious and scholarly studies, plots were being hatched and battles fought out on the other side of the monastery walls. These involved complex intrigues between warlords of the central provinces of U and Tsang, and between Lhassa and Shigatse. These were sometimes settled by the intervention of Mongol chieftains. The Dalai Lama finally came forward to offer his own mediation, which inspired the Mongol conqueror to proclaim him the supreme authority over all Tibet, from the region of Dartsedo (Tsatsienlu) in the east to the border of Ladakh in the west.

In 1645, the fifth Dalai Lama reconstructed the Potala and established his government there, making Lhassa the capital. His character was one of great courage and determination—and he was endowed with a rare political shrewdness—all qualities which were extremely important for the survival of Tibet in those days, when its territory was constantly a temptation for both Mongol and Chinese appetites. There were intermittent troubles in the Ladakh area, as in Bhutan and Sikkim; yet these fires were rapidly extinguished, thanks to his skill. He also undertook a voyage to Peking at the request of the Manchu ruler. On this occasion, the Yellow Palace of the Forbidden City was built especially for the great Tibetan lama.

In addition, he was a man of immense erudition in the most secret tantras, and spared no effort in his plan of providing tantric instruction to the most gifted of his subjects. He was open and tolerant with regard to religious beliefs different from his own, and favorable towards cultural exchanges with India. He also encouraged great works of translation of fundamental Buddhist texts, editing some of them himself. To assure a harmonious administration of his country, he surrounded himself with the most competent and devoted ministers, trained especially for their posts. He died in 1682 at the age of sixty-eight, but his death was not publicly revealed until a dozen years later. This information was withheld so as to have time to complete the reconstruction of the Potala, to discourage outside enemies from adventures, and to maintain internal stability. And there was also the need to find his new incarnation.

Very different from his predecessor, the sixth Dalai Lama began to distinguish himself very early by his eccentricities and provocative behavior, to the dismay of the religious dignitaries around him. A skillful archer, a lover of drinking songs and pretty girls, gifted in poetry, and apparently not overly concerned with his spiritual duties, the sixth Dalai Lama has gone down in Tibetan history primarily as a great poet. In spite of the admonitions and threats of the lamas, including his tutors, he refused to take full monastic vows, yet also insisted on retaining full powers of office.

At the age of twenty-four, the young, worldly, and rebellious Dalai Lama was made a prisoner by the Mongol Khan, who saw himself as guardian of the religion, with the intention of removing him from office. While on the road to probable exile in Mongolia or China, Tsangyang Gyatso died mysteriously—legend has it that he was taken away by a whirlwind not far from the blue waters of Kukunor. No place of burial has ever been known.

Much confusion followed this strange episode, aggravating the wars between Mongols and Manchus, while a seventh Dalai Lama was being enthroned. This *tulku* proved to be a true scholar, but his political power was limited. Rivalries and intrigues multiplied around him, fueled by the personal ambitions of a headstrong regent. After the regent's death, the Dalai Lama instituted a council of ministers known as the *kashag*,[13] so as to correct and dilute the excessive political power which had fallen into the hands of this regent.

For the next hundred years or so, up until 1876, the eighth, ninth, tenth, eleventh, and twelfth Dalai Lamas followed each other in very rapid succession. Strangely, none of them survived much into maturity, nor had the time to impose any personal stamp upon national developments. They all died young, either from disease or from unfortunate accidents, leaving the field open to increasingly clandestine manipulations in the back corridors of power. A persistent rumor had it that one or another of the incarnations had clumsily offended the very redoubtable Palden Lhamo, protective divinity of the lineage. But still other rumors blamed evil sorcerers, poisoning by cooks, or criminals in their entourage, tempted by power and riches.

This led to a long period of conflict, instability, and murderous political intrigues, with disastrous consequences for the country as a whole. Manchu power now began to roll back the Mongol influence which had covered all of Himalayan Asia. It began to gain

---

[13]*Kashag* is the Tibetan council of ministers.

influence in Tibet, where its emissaries, the *ambans*,[14] held roles of power. Yet this power was subject to great fluctuations according to which alliances or armed powers held sway at the moment. On the other hand, the atmosphere of plotting and power-struggle in the monasteries began to die down, making it seem as if the anger of the goddess had begun to calm somewhat.

In 1876, with the birth of the thirteenth Dalai Lama, the gods were not the only ones to offer guidance in searching for the true *tulku,* and other distinctly more worldly influences vied with each other for influence around the cradle. During these years of the end of the nineteenth century, upheavals were going on which were to have decisive implications for Asia as well as for Europe. Without intending it, and almost unknowingly, Tibet found itself caught in the crossfire between British and Russian imperial ambitions, whereas the Chinese empire was festering with resentments and desires for vengeance against European power.

Manipulating alliances, treaties, agreements, and occasionally resorting to violence and deceptive manipulations, British power consolidated and protected its base among the maharajas and other local powers of the Indian subcontinent. Its emissaries began methodically establishing bases in the Himalayan foothills, using the institution of the "Protectorate" in Ladakh, Sikkim, and the borders of Bhutan. Yet Tibetan power was oblivious to these implications, sheltered (as it believed it was) by the great mountain barriers. It did not notice the growing interest in its affairs by increasingly numerous travelers there, often under the cover of pilgrims, missionaries, explorers, or traders.

Meanwhile Czarist power was moving steadily beyond the Urals into the great spaces of central Asia, often thanks to intrepid expeditions which united military expertise and scientific and cultural

---

[14] *Amban* is historically a Chinese envoy or ambassador to Lhassa. Their role and powers varied greatly, according to circumstances: from simple diplomats at one period, to powerful decision-makers in Tibetan affairs during another.

curiosity. After the first Afghanistan war, they took control of the vast territory from the Caspian to Turkestan and the Pamir, right to the banks of the Amur Darya river, which began to infringe upon domains jealously held by the Manchus. Kalmuk and Buryat merchants who had long been Buddhists via Mongol influence, became useful intermediaries used by Russian power to gain information about the mysteries of the Land of Snows. In 1880, Agvan Dorje, a Buryat lama, undertook a pilgrimage to Lhassa where he quickly acquired a major reputation and influence. Some years later he would become still better known for other reasons under the Russianized name of Dorjiev.

With the weakening of the central Manchu power in Peking, the influence of their *ambans* also waned in Lhassa. The Sino-Japanese war of 1894–95 was the first rude blow to the pride of the Sons of Heaven. As Lobsang Thubten Gyatso, the thirteenth Dalai Lama, was just taking on the direction of his country, Tibet and Britain came into conflict over Sikkim. A young and brilliant monk with a strong character, the new sovereign was endowed with both lively curiosity and a sound political intuition, all the more extraordinary for his lack of experience of the world beyond Tibet. The son of a modest peasant family of the hamlet of Langdun, near the Mountain of the Elephant, he soon had to deal with major challenges.

Lord Curzon, Viceroy of India, was exasperated by the refusal of the authorities at Lhassa to credit his representatives, and even more so by rumors of an alliance between the Potala and the Czarist court, engineered by Dorjiev. In 1904 he dispatched an expedition into the high plateaus, commanded by Colonel Francis Younghusband. This was a clear sign that Tibet now lay in the sphere of both British and Russian ambitions, with Peking momentarily in retreat.

Anxious to avoid any danger to their precious Master, Tibetan officials sent him with great ceremony to Urga in Mongolia, where he lived for over a year. He then left to visit several monasteries in Tibet, taking stock of the overall situation in the provinces of his kingdom, and then received an invitation to visit Peking. He finally accepted it, but refrained from appearing in an audience before the Emperor, so as not to be required to prostrate himself before the latter as protocol would have required. An interview was nevertheless arranged with the dowager Empress. It turned out that the Dalai Lama was destined to attend both their funerals before leaving Peking in 1908, the day following the coronation of (as it turned out) the last ruler of the Manchu dynasty.

During this long voyage, Russia and Great Britain signed agreements concerning their conflicting Asian interests, without even bothering to consult the countries involved, including Afghanistan, Persia, and Tibet. British diplomacy at this time was incapable of seeing beyond short-term interests, and was especially blind to the disastrous long-term consequences for Tibet of British heedlessness of the Chinese threat. While residing in China, and also en route during his voyage there, the Dalai Lama had met a number of foreign diplomats, especially the American W.W. Rockhill, the Russian Colonel von Mannerheim, a Japanese lieutenant-general attached to the embassy, and a German officer. He also met the son of the Maharaja of Sikkim, and committed himself to sponsor a restoration of Buddhist holy sites in India.

Upon his return to Lhassa in 1909, the Dalai Lama found the capital in great disorder, especially because of the demands of the Chinese *ambans* and their collaborators. Chaos already reigned within the provinces of Kham and Amdo, which had been taken over by Chinese warlords who ruled with terror, torture, and forced annexations. Troubles multiplied still further with the announcement that the army of Chao Erfeng was planning to march upon Lhassa.

The Dalai Lama then appealed to the British crown and to the Nepalese embassy, who attempted negotiations with the Chinese emissaries. But these failed, and faced with the imminent arrival of Chinese troops, he quickly left the Potala in February, 1910, seeking refuge in India. After a pilgrimage to Benares, to Sarnath, and to major Buddhist holy places, he settled for two years in Darjeeling.

It was here that he began his important friendship with Charles Bell, later to become British resident envoy in Tibet. We owe much to the latter for our knowledge of Tibet in those times.

During this time the Chinese in Lhassa were running up against a determined resistance by the people, led by the Dalai Lama's appointed provisional directors. An Imperial edict destituting the Dalai Lama of his powers was publicly defiled and torn, and the Panchen Lama refused to cooperate with the Chinese by taking the place of the absent sovereign. The Tibetan assembly also refused to collaborate. Meanwhile the Manchu dynasty began to be shaken by its final convulsions: the revolution of 1911 brought an end to it, and the first Chinese Republic was officially declared soon thereafter.

In his growing experience of the workings of the modern world in British-occupied India, the Dalai Lama was not long in grasping the extent of its cynicism and vanity, as well as the unreliability of its promises and its signed agreements. At last the time came when he was able to return home to a capital which had been rid of the last Chinese soldier. In 1912 he signed the Treaty of Urga with Mongolia, recognizing the full sovereignty of the two countries. He also officially reaffirmed Tibet's status as an independent nation in a solemn international declaration published in Lhassa in early 1913.

Very soon after his return, the thirteenth Dalai Lama began to institute major reforms, some of which offended prominent families and others, including a rather conservative Buddhist clergy. Apparently keenly aware of the future danger to Tibet, he created a high army command, increased troop strength, and attempted to modernize his weaponry. This did not go over so well in a conservative society which traditionally recognized brigand tribal chieftains as having their place in the world, and yet had little or no respect for the military profession itself. He also opened secular schools, and sent young students abroad for a modern education, actions which stirred up considerable mistrust and even resistance among the lamas, who saw this as undermining their own authority.

He set up an authority for training policemen and maintaining public order, a mint to replace the Chinese coins still in general use, had postage stamps made, and began construction of a regular postal and telegraph service. It also fell to him to establish the first Office of Foreign Affairs that Tibet had ever known. All this will towards innovation, reform, and adaptation to changing times began to cause more and more friction among the short-sighted and backward-looking elite classes of Tibetan society. The most upsetting of all these changes was the levying of new taxes, which caused hostility in the monasteries and among the nobility. And his already difficult task was further complicated by instabilities outside the country.

Although he was able to keep a firm grip on the reins of power until his death in 1933, Thubten Gyatso saw himself forced to keep an equal distance from Great Britain and from China, aware though he was of the greater danger from the latter. He seems to have been ahead of his time in his understanding of the impossibility of Tibet continuing its age-old isolationist policies, under the illusion of being protected by the Himalayas. This also included a keen awareness of internal changes which would be necessary if Tibet were to have any chances of surviving as an independent country in the newly emerging geopolitical reality.

The passing of the thirteenth Dalai Lama in such an unstable international context left the field open to all sorts of conflicting interests, and the ensuing atmosphere of petty power struggles among clans and other political factions was one in which his prophetic warnings went mostly unheeded. Tibet was destined to undergo hideous sufferings before belatedly realizing the full measure of his wisdom.[15]

---

[15] For a striking documentation of this, see the "Testament of the Thirteenth Dalai Lama," appendixed here.

On the Roof of the Potala

The installation of the new sovereign *tulku* upon the Throne of the Lion did not clean the corridors of power of their intrigues. The fourteenth Gyalwa Rinpoche, a title signifying "Precious Victory," turned out to be an extraordinarily gifted child, something which his country badly needed. Yet he was still but a child, and the responsibilities which already cried out for his attention were too heavy for his tender age. The regent, Reting Rinpoche, was handling the transition, and unfortunately the regency of the fourteenth Dalai Lama was no exception to the general rule of plots and palace intrigues which had so often typified such periods.

While the child sovereign lived at the summer palace of Norbulingka, not yet submitted to strict monastic discipline, and while the rest of his family were settling in, life outside the fortress walls of Tibet followed its own course. The year of 1939 resounded with the faraway echoes of war in Europe, and in 1940 it was already becoming clear that these events would have serious consequences for the new ruler of Tibet.

Those first months spent at the summer palace remain among the happiest memories of the fourteenth Dalai Lama. This period, which he himself qualifies as "carefree," was filled with long walks, games, and family gatherings. Naturally he was closely supervised in all he did, but in an atmosphere of good humor. The regent preferred to allow the child greater freedom for now, while awaiting the propitious moment (to be determined by astrologers and oracles) for his official entry into monastic life.

The Dalai Lama recounts one very precise memory of this period, in which he had to miss one of Tibet's most important festivals: the *Losar,* or new year. On this occasion, great ceremonies and festivities were being organized at the Potala. However, because the right moment had not yet been declared for the enthronement of the child, it was thought better for him not to attend. His mother and brother, Lobsang Samten, were nevertheless invited, and Tenzin Gyatso remembers his rage and frustration after their return, upon hearing his brother give a detailed account of the luscious food and the splendid ritual dances known as *sham,* with their extravagant masks and costumes.

Because he was not yet ordained, he took advantage, without being fully aware of it, of certain indulgences such as eggs or pork fritters; food which was strictly forbidden to monks. His mother was an excellent cook, and made sure he had plenty of the cookies, little pastries, and other treats which he loved.

This relative freedom was not to last long, and the date of enthronement was solemnly fixed as the fourteenth day of the first month of the Iron Dragon (February 22, 1940). About two months after his arrival in Lhassa, Lhamo Thondup—the name given him at birth, and which placed him under protection of a powerful goddess—had been led with great pomp before the statue of Jowo Shakyamuni Buddha, where the regent proceeded with the ceremony of shaving the child's head, formally marking his entry into the orders. On this same occasion, he received his new monastic name of Jamphel Ngawang Lobsang Yeshe Tenzin Gyatso, which summarized the qualities he was to manifest: the Very Glorious one with mastery over himself; the Great Compassionate One, Master of the Faith, Powerful in Word, Pure in Spirit, and endowed with Divine Wisdom. And of course, as had been said long ago by the Mongol disciple: Ocean of Wisdom. Besides these, there were other traditional names often used by Tibetans to refer to a Dalai Lama: Gyalwa Rinpoche is the most popular, meaning Precious Victorious One. Others include the Lord of the White Lotus, the Wish-fulfilling

Jewel, Precious Knowledge, Incomparable Master... or simply, Kundun, meaning the Presence.

Now official letters of declaration were sent out by the *kashag* to the British government of India, to Peking, to the King of Nepal, as well as to the Maharajas of Sikkim and Bhutan. Their emissaries also attended the ceremonies at Lhassa, welcomed with highest honors and in the greatest Oriental pomp and luxury—yet carefully treated with equal rank among each other. Witnesses to the scene were unanimous in their impression of the noble and faultless bearing of the child, of his remarkable ease in his role, which he carried out with no signs of fatigue or boredom as would be expected in one so young.

Raised for the first time to the Throne of the Lion, Tenzin Gyatso remembers the countless precious jewels imbedded in its wood, in the hall of Si-Shi-Phuntsok, known as the hall of "all blessings of spiritual and temporal worlds" in the Potala. Besides the personal seals of his lineage, he was also given the Golden Wheel and the White Conch, symbolizing temporal and spiritual powers. In principle, he would not be allowed to exercise the former until the age of eighteen, devoting himself in the meantime to the perfection of his training. From then on he would be considered as the supreme and most revered master of the land, to whom each subject owed obedience and loyalty. In exchange, he promised his protection and justice for all.

Around 1850, the distinguished traveler Father Huc wrote of his visit to the Tibetan capital:

> Lha-Ssa is not a large city. Its circumference is at most two leagues. It is not completely surrounded by ramparts, as are Chinese cities. Among the suburbs one finds a large number of gardens with great trees, which make a magnificent greenery all around the city. The main streets of Lha-Ssa are quite wide, well laid-out, and clean. [...] The palace of the

Talé-Lama entirely deserves its world-wide fame. Near the northern part of the city there is a small rocky mountain of conical form. It rises high up in the midst of a wide valley, like an island over a vast lake. This mountain bears the name of Buddha-la, or "mountain of Buddha." It is upon this grandiose foundation that the Talé-Lama's devotees have built a magnificent palace, where their incarnate divinity resides in flesh and blood.[16]

About a century later, Amaury de Riencourt recounted his arrival there in 1947:

As we drew near to Lhassa, the enormous bulk of the Potala loomed even greater. Mentally comparing its dimensions with those of some of the greatest palaces of the world I had visited, I came to the conclusion that the Spanish Escorial and the English Windsor seemed little more than cottages beside this astounding Vatican of the Buddhist world.[17]

An American journalist who traveled through the City of the Gods in 1951 wrote of the Potala:

What really takes one's breath away are the immense proportions and grandeur of its façade, simple and almost austere though it is, as well as the way its foundations seem to grow naturally out of the rock. It is difficult to say where the mountain ends and the building begins. The Potala is about 900 feet long and over 800 feet high, and contains 12 stories. Its height is about two-thirds that of the Empire State Building of New York. In fact, it reminds one of an American skyscraper in the way it hovers over the city of Lhassa.

---

[16] R.P. Huc, "Dans le Thibet," *Souvenirs d'aun voyage dans la Tartarie, le Thibet, et la Chine,* vol. II (Paris: Librairie Plon, 1926).

[17] A. de Riencourt, *Le Toit du monde* (Paris: France-Empire, 1955).

Surrounded by dignitaries.

The Potala contains over a thousand rooms. Below are storage spaces, government offices, kitchens, and lodgings for about 200–300 monks. The two principal treasuries of Tibet are also located there. One of them, the *trédé*, is exclusively reserved for the use of the Dalai Lamas. The other serves to cover expenses for war or other urgencies. There is also a prison there, as well as the private monastery of the Dalai Lamas. Higher up one finds chapels, audience and reception halls, libraries, and the tombs of the Dalai Lamas.

Still higher up are the private apartments of the Dalai Lama, along with those of his counselors and servants.[18]

Yet the great red and white palace also evokes other types of impressions, as noted by F. Spencer Chapman, a high British official who spent time in the Tibetan capital in 1936–37:

For me, the Potala represents the very essence of the Tibetan people. It manifests a sort of untamed dignity, in perfect harmony with the wilderness surrounding it, a quality of imperturbable everlastingness. It seems to say: "I have been here for centuries, and I intend to abide here forever." [...] The Potala is certainly one of the most astonishing edifices on earth, whether seen from a distance, perched upon a promontory arising straight out of the plain of Lhassa, in the sunlight which illumines its golden roofs and high pavilions; or whether it is seen as it emerges out of the pre-dawn darkness as the moonlight bathes the white wall of its immense southern face with an unreal brilliance. All the greatest works of art, literature, painting, and architecture possess an indefinable quality of magic, which usually arises from circumstances beyond the control of the artist. Exactly as with a few other indisputably perfect buildings in the world, the Potala

---

[18] Lowell Thomas, Jr., *Out of this World* (London: Macdonald & Co., 1951).

possesses a transcendental quality whose origins can be found neither in the inspired skill of its builders, nor in its historical associations, nor even in its role as the focal point of numberless acts of devotion. It has that divine excellence which simply cannot be denied. [...]

The Potala gives the impression of not having been built by human hands, but of having grown there, so perfectly does it fit its environment. It adorns itself in that same agreeable lack of symmetry possessed by a great tree or a majestic mountain. And yet this apparent banality is first concentrated in the red block at the center, and subsequently in the golden pavilions of the roof, so that one's gaze is naturally directed from the less important to the essential, both visually and spiritually. Just as the golden roofs which shelter the mortal remains of the Dalai Lamas form such a dominant architectural feature, so the spirit of these incarnate masters is the true soul of Tibet.[19]

A decade later, Heinrich Harrer wrote:

Tibet is a country with a powerful history. As one indication, consider the stone obelisk dating from 763 C.E., raised to commemorate their military victories over the Chinese. The Tibetan army reached the very gates of the Chinese capital, and imposed an annual tribute of fifty thousand rolls of silk as a sign of fealty. But little by little, this national warrior temperament was becoming transformed into one of mysticism. The Potala, both temple and fortress, dates from this transitional period. One day I asked a tailor why he thought the Tibetans did not continue in their ancestors' tradition, and build other great monuments such as this, and he replied: "But the Potala was made by gods, not by men. During the

---

[19] F. Spencer Chapman, *Lhasa, the Holy City* (London: Reader Union Ltd., 1940).

night, spirits came and built it. Men could never have made such a marvelous thing."[20]

The young fourteenth Dalai Lama could not have been fully aware of the nature of the grandeur he lived in. For him, the years which followed were filled with intense study and solitude. As a novice, he began to learn reading and writing on wooden tablets, painstaking memorizations of canonical scriptures and philosophical texts, as well as the practice of meditation. These rigorous hours were first shared with Lobsang Samten, but the two brothers were so full of energy that their rambunctious uproar disturbed the austere calm of the palace. Shortly afterward, his brother was sent to a private school, and Tenzin Gyatso found himself more alone than ever in preparing for his future.

The Dalai Lama has little to say about this period, important though it was in his education. Considering himself as a "simple Buddhist monk," he feels he has nothing of importance to say about this subject—in any case, a basic teaching of Buddhism discourages any sort of display of one's personal realizations or attainments. It is one's way of being and relating to others on a daily basis that bears true witness as to how far one has traveled upon the Way. The authentic sage has no need to make himself known: he simply is, and his behavior speaks for him.

However, the Dalai Lama has occasionally touched upon this period, although only in the most general and illustrative terms:

> I studied Buddhism in my own language, and became a monk at a very young age. In fact, the environment was especially favorable for me. On a more personal level, it was only at the age of fifteen or sixteen that I began to experience a veritable enthusiasm for the practice. Since then, I have never ceased to practice. The will to practice with unbroken effort

[20] H. Harrer, *Seven Years in Tibet*, 1953, 1997. This book was the basis of the recent film *Kundun*, by Martin Scorcese, about the young Dalai Lama.

is of primary importance. Inner development happens step by step, and progress follows from the constancy of daily effort.[21]

Thubten Jigme Norbu, the Dalai Lama's eldest brother, and a monk since childhood himself (he was recognized as the *tulku* of the Lama of Taktser), was about seventeen years old when he followed his family to Lhassa. His memories of this period are of interest:

> After my arrival, I spent time with my family, though the Gyalwa Rinpoche of course had very limited leisure time to spend with us. I was also sent to visit Lhassa as any pilgrim does, performing my devotions in the holy places, and I was a curious tourist there as well. I was allowed to frequent the most elevated social circles, which I would have never dreamed of back in Amdo. Yet I saw little or nothing in them which seemed to inspire much respect, still less desire.
>
> No one should demand any special respect for having accomplished their duty, and those whom fortune has caused to be born in the noble classes have their own duties, just as we do. In Lhassa, politics is full of intrigue and manipulation just as it is everywhere. Contrary to a widespread belief, our government is not entirely, but only half composed of monks. The rest are laity.[22]

Indeed there was no lack of intrigue in the small but turbulent world of Tibetan politics, both religious and secular. Shortly after the enthronement of Tenzin Gyatso, several oracles warned the regent that his days were numbered, unless he withdrew from public life

---

[21] Claude B. Levenson, *Le Seigneur du Lotus blanc* (Paris: Livre de Poche, 1989).

[22] Thubten Jigme Norbu and Colin Turnbull, *Tibet, its History, Religion and People* (New York: Penguin, 1969).

and devoted himself to prayer and meditation. Reting Rinpoche gave in to this, partly because his reputation had already suffered from rumors in the city and in the monasteries. He had especially been criticized for having broken his vows of celibacy and having done nothing to stop corruption, including the nepotism which afflicted his administration. He retired, yielding his place to Taktra Rinpoche, the Dalai Lama's second preceptor, who was highly respected because of his spiritual qualities. Kewtsang Rinpoche, who had led the search party to the humble farm of the village of Taktser, was now also part of the close entourage of the young Dalai Lama.

During these years of transition, the interplay of foreign influences continued, manifesting themselves in significances which clearly escaped the understanding of Tibetan leaders—apparently they were still little able, or willing, to understand the changing realities of the outside world. Shortly after the changing of the regent, the upheavals of the Second World War began to affect even the Himalayan world. The Japanese offensive cut off the Burmese route which had served as a link between India and China. Indian and Chinese officials then sought to open an alternative military route which would pass through the Zayul, in southeastern Tibet.

In Lhassa, the chief officer of the Chinese delegation and the head of the British mission, acting as spokesmen for their respective governments, demanded authorization for this road from the Tibetan Foreign Affairs Office, which then put the request to the *kashag*, who in turn passed it to Taktra Rinpoche. The latter decided to refer it to the *tsongdu*, the national assembly, which only met to consider urgent questions of national interest. Chinese threats and British pressure did not intimidate them, and the *tsongdu* refused to allow the passage of military material through Tibetan territory, explaining to the British that Tibet desired to maintain its neutrality. However, so as not to further embarrass the British masters of India, a permit was granted for the transport of non-military material through Tibet towards China.

Some months later, unexpected messengers made their way to the Potala: Captain Ilya Tolstoy, and Lieutenant Brooke Dolan, both from U.S. military intelligence, had been officially dispatched there to seek a passage for convoys for a supply route to China. For the first time ever, an American envoy was received as such in the Tibetan capital, and granted an audience with the Dalai Lama. A very formal exchange of letters and presents between President Roosevelt and the young sovereign crowned the event. The two Americans were ceremoniously accompanied by Tibetan officials to Shining, at the Chinese border, to pursue their mission further.

However, even though the personal seal of the Dalai Lama appeared on the document of February 24, 1943, sent to the President of the United States, the young sovereign was not really that involved in such affairs. Under the severe yet benevolent regard of his masters, he still spent most of his time studying and learning— or rather, in refreshing his memory, according to some who worked directly with him in those days—for Tenzin Gyatso learned even the most difficult texts with an amazing rapidity, according to his teachers. The lessons took place in halls devoted especially to this purpose, one in the Potala, and the other at Norbulingka. Yet the daily routine was essentially the same.

At dawn, waking was followed by toilette, first prayer, and first meditation. Breakfast, consisting of tea and *tsampa* (a barley flour dish which is the basis of the Tibetan diet) sweetened with honey or sugared candy, was taken afterwards. Then came the first lesson of the day, devoted to reading and writing. Afterward came memory exercises, and the learning of scriptures by heart. A brief recreation, and then current affairs: the regent and ministers appeared with files to discuss with him, civil servants completed their reports, or sometimes referred delicate cases to him. But during this period of apprenticeship, these discussions were more ceremony than substance, and the most important decisions were still made by others.

After these administrative formalities, his other preceptor came and had his student repeat the texts memorized earlier that morning. Finally midday arrived, announced by a cry from the conch shell and the ringing of a bell. For the child in the Dalai Lama, this was also a time of deliverance, an all-too-brief time when he was free to play and relax. Household servants now held privilege of place in his austere existence, except for the times after his younger brother Tenzin Chögyal was old enough to come with his mother to visit him. But for the young Gyalwa Rinpoche, her visits were never as frequent as he would have liked.

From these years, the fourteenth Dalai Lama also remembers the gifts brought by foreign visitors. The pair of singing birds and the golden watch given him by Roosevelt are well-remembered, but especially appreciated was the game of Meccano (similar to the American "Erector Set") offered by the head of the British mission to Lhassa, which afforded him countless hours of enthusiastic absorption. He also enjoyed examining the dusty gifts left for his predecessors, where he discovered a number of small treasures: ancient watches, music boxes, rusty mechanical toys. During this time he developed a passion for tinkering with mechanical devices, and became quite adept in dismantling, reassembling, and even repairing them.

On the other hand, the beautiful silk cloths sent by the Chinese authorities left him indifferent. What was he to do with them? He did enjoy the crates of apples which were sometimes sent by an official from the Indian border, and many moments of amusement were afforded by a miniature train of unknown origin. The future apostle of peace even played for awhile with a set of lead soldiers, and he tried to sculpt tanks and airplanes out of dried *tsampa* meal. However, a few years later he carefully melted down this military company, passing them through the fire and then transforming them into a community of monks!

Studies recommenced in the afternoon after a light lunch, but the child had trouble concentrating on the scholarly texts. The daily exercises in debate captured more of his attention until tea-time, which preceded practical exercise in philosophical discussion.

Before the evening meal, Tenzin Gyatso spent some time outdoors, often upon his private walkway over the Potala rooftops, from where he liked to observe Lhassa and its inhabitants through a telescope he had discovered in the jumbled possessions of his predecessors. He remembers a sadness at being unable to join in the activities and games he saw young peasants playing, as they returned home in groups, often singing, to the village of Shol at the foot of his great palace. At other times he would follow from afar the lines of prisoners working at the foot of the hill. Once when they saw and recognized him standing on the roof, they all prostrated themselves...

Other than these distant companions whom he only visited in his imagination, the young Dalai Lama made easy alliances with those in his service. Besides his masters and mentors, whose relations with him were largely influenced by ancient custom, he had always manifested an attention to those around him which was free of all presumption or prejudice. Whether innate or cultivated, this quality is one of his major characteristics, and is often noticed by people of very different backgrounds who meet him today. He himself has remarked that his early associations with people of humble background were an excellent preparation for learning to appreciate human relationships and beings for their real value.

The janitors of the Potala, Norbulingka, and the Jokhang were often former soldiers of poor families. This did not prevent him from engaging them as partners in play. When he needed adversaries for his epic battles of toy soldiers, he knew he could count on them. Yet once the combat had begun, nothing else mattered. Dalai Lama or not, these companions wanted to win just as badly as he did, and sometimes he would be seen shaking with rage when he lost.

Sometimes these companions disappointed him in a more serious way, though. Some months after one of his first stays in his private apartments at the Jokhang sanctuary, he inquired as to the absence of some of the servants he had enjoyed playing with there after his religious duties for the day were over. He still remembers

49

the sadness he felt upon learning that after his departure, several of those he had taken for friends had broken into his rooms and stolen several precious objects, including ritual bowls and other items reserved for his exclusive use. The guilty ones had been simply dismissed with no further ado.

Most days, the arrival of darkness signaled the time for the evening meal. Ordinarily, a Buddhist monk is supposed to take no solid food after midday, but this observance is not strictly required of youthful novices who still need food for physical growth. Yet the menu varied little: there was always tea, and usually soup and yogurt. Sometimes a bit of meat was to be had, and occasional special breads made for him by his mother.

The Dalai Lama shared these Spartan suppers with his companions, sometimes with his servant friends, other times with a visiting abbot from his private Namgyal monastery within the Potala, and most often with the three monks permanently attached to his service. Although he did not particularly welcome visits from taciturn superiors whose presence had a dampening effect on laughter and jokes, he remembers some beautiful moments during winter suppers near the fire, while snowstorms and other invisible menaces raged outside the palace walls.

When good weather came, this child so full of energy and so surrounded with adult attention, yet so alone in his vast palace, was finally allowed some outdoor recreation. Yet even then, while enjoying the fresh air of the interior courtyard, he was expected to continue repeating sacred texts and prayers. The Dalai Lama confesses that for a long time, he only pretended to repeat the texts, and instead invented stories, or repeated others he had heard, even editing and arranging them skillfully, so as to make them dramatic and even frightening. He sometimes went so far in this that he remembers being so distressed by these stories that he feared the moment of having to return alone to his dark rooms up high, to the bedroom where his predecessors had lived, where the dust of years had so long collected that mice and other vermin were to be heard moving above his canopied bed. Since the Himalayan imagination is far from lacking in traditions of fantastic creatures of supernatural powers, it did not take much for these vermin to become colored monsters which invaded his dreams, until he finally learned to master them.

The heroic tales of Gesar Ling, which enrich Tibetan memory with exploits and great legends, are linked in the Dalai Lama's memory with that of an old bard who used to come to the Potala and make these flamboyant myths come alive especially for him.

> There was a marvelous storyteller who sometimes came to tell me these fabulous legends. I loved listening to him, and was deeply impressed by him. Do you know why? It was not only because he knew a multitude of details and variations, probably adding some inventions of his own, but also because he had this immense bowl of tea, really huge. He would fill it copiously with endless quantities of the brew, which he gulped down with amazing ease. Just imagine—it was part of his salary, and also his obvious delight: to drink huge quantities of tea from the kitchens of the Dalai Lama![23]

During these years certain regular practices were introduced which shaped—or reaffirmed?—the deepest foundations of his personality. These meditation retreats, which Tibetans say have existed since time immemorial, beginningless and endless, both reflect and inform the life and being of the Dalai Lama. At first he had little liking for these austere three-week periods which came in winter before the festival of the new year. During this time his only company was a tutor or an old lama—and that was only once a day for a lesson. The rest of the time he had to remain inside, so alone in silence and meditation that it might sometimes have resembled solitary confinement in prison.

---

[23] Claude B. Levenson, *Le Seigneur du Lotus blanc* (Paris: Livre de Poche, 1989).

Between meditation and prayers, his only distraction lay in gazing outside through the windows. On one side lay the monastery of Sera in the distance, perched upon the mountain with its hermitages, residence halls, and golden roofs. On the other side his gaze would run tirelessly over the series of *thangka*[24] paintings displayed on the walls of the government meeting hall which was next to his retreat space. These ornate paintings on silk recounted the life of Milarepa, the ascetic poet revered all over the Himalayas, and whose poetry still permeates both popular and erudite Tibetan culture. At the present time, no one seems to know what has become of these treasures of art in the traumatic events of Tibet's recent history.

Gifted with an excellent memory and submitted to a rigorous discipline, this Dalai Lama got along well with his teachers, because he learned so quickly. Yet he admits that he was content to make the minimum effort necessary. This did not go unnoticed by Sherab Tenzin, one of the three monks attached to his service, who had also been part of the mission of discovery at Taktser, and who now taught him literature. Sherab deplored this nonchalance of his gifted young protégé, yet his remonstrances had no effect on him. Finally, in order to put a bit more spice in his studies, he proposed that the young Dalai Lama have a competition with one of his janitor friends. The idea of having a contest with one of his favorite companions amused him, yet he was unaware that Sherab Tenzin had already been secretly at work to prepare the other youth for the match. To his great surprise and acute embarrassment, the little monk saw himself soundly defeated by the skillful answers of his adversary. Yet he felt no resentment when he learned of the trick, and in fact it had the desired effect of inspiring him to work harder at his studies. But this only lasted for a time, and he soon returned to his old insouciance. He has written himself of this subject:

---

[24] *Thangka* is a Tibetan Buddhist religious painting, typically large, extravagantly colored, and in mandala form, depicting many types of divinities and sages.

It was only when I became an adult that I truly understood the importance of learning, and began to cultivate myself seriously. Today I feel some remorse for this laziness of my youth, and I spend about four hours a day at my studies. One thing that was no doubt lacking in my upbringing was the stimulation of an appropriate model whom I could emulate.[25]

The young Dalai Lama also found time to develop his aptitude for mechanics during this period, as he rummaged and explored among the storage rooms of the Potala, where the possessions of his predecessors were like a tremendous treasure for the solitary child. One day he stumbled upon two dusty wheels, whose use he soon deduced: they were film reels. He found the projector, but had no idea how it worked. Yet his perseverance was as intense as his youthful eagerness, and at the age of nine he finally discovered an ancient monk at the Norbulingka palace who knew the secret.

This man was a Chinese who had been given into the thirteenth Dalai Lama's service in 1908 during the latter's visit to the court of the Emperor at Peking. Ever since then, he had lived quietly at the summer palace, a harmless old man filled with obscure memories. It was this monk who initiated the new master of Tibet into the mysteries of the generator and the mechanical operation of the movie projector, shortly before taking final leave of an earthly life which seemed to have little more interest for him. Although the Dalai Lama admits that the old man's character was a rather difficult one ("like many Chinese," he adds), he remembers him with gratitude, and has never forgotten the intense pleasure of his very first experience of a movie: a film of the coronation of George VI of England.

Yet the young Tenzin Gyatso was more deeply impressed by another film, which he still remembers vividly: a documentary about the mining and extraction of gold. This film awakened his compassion for the dangerous lives led by miners, and it was from this

---

[25] Tenzin Gyatso, *Au loin la liberté* (Paris: Fayard, 1990).

time on that he began to develop a keen awareness of the plight of working-class people. The images and long reflections elicited by this film were what enabled him to give his own concrete meaning to political discourse he was often to encounter in the future, which spoke of "exploitation of the working classes," etc. Even before this, he had always had a real sympathy and interest in simple people, and took great pleasure in observing the daily lives of his subjects on those all-too-rare occasions when he was allowed the liberty of excursions among them.

There was another incident during these years, which should have been a clear sign to the young sovereign's advisors that their lives in the high Himalayan plateaus would be altered forever by major forces in the outside world, and that swift response was needed if these changes were not to be destructive. Yet this sign went just as unheeded as the warnings of the thirteenth Dalai Lama in his 1933 testament *(see appendix)*.

Tibet's directors were apparently too complacent in their isolation, and too little aware of the technological mutations which had altered the very nature of war, to understand the full implications of the object which literally fell from the sky in 1944. The airplane's commander, Lieutenant R.E. Crozier, had gone astray on a supply mission from India to China. Having run out of fuel, he crash-landed near the Samye monastery not far from Lhassa. Welcomed and cared for, the team was later escorted to the Indian border. The American diplomatic mission in India thanked the Tibetans for their hospitality, and promised not to fly any more aircraft over Tibetan territory. The Tibetan government did at least draw the conclusion that it might not be such a bad idea after all for some officials to begin to learn English, as the previous Dalai Lama had advocated in vain so many years ago...

An English school was finally opened in Lhassa, with the aim of providing a different kind of training for local aristocrats destined for a governmental career. But this caused mounting agitation in the monasteries around the capital, where some were worried about the bad effects these new foreign ideas might have upon religious beliefs. This was of course a virtual repeat of the scenario of 1923, and the reaction to his imposition of English courses at the Gyantse school, which at that time was the primary British commercial office in Tibet. That school had been able to last for three years—but the new one was closed within months, and its students sent to study in Sikkim and in India.

Much more would have to happen before these diviners of subtle signs and powers of the Roof of the World finally began to understand the stark implications of the strange upheavals taking place in the barbaric countries beyond the mountain walls. Only distant echoes reached their ears, and by the time they began to understand their meaning, it was too late. The new Dalai Lama would have to learn how to deal with these events mostly on his own, in one of the harshest of life's schools: that of exile, and powerlessness to prevent mass suffering among his people.

A Traveler on the Way

According to Tibetan belief, one doesn't become a Dalai Lama, because the Dalai Lama already *is*. In spite of the diversity of incarnated personalities, there is only one. His different names reflect the radiance of different qualities, as symbolized by the traditional iconography which often shows an aura with thousands of pairs of arms. Tibetan tradition holds that the Dalai Lama is not a human being just like anyone else, but the vehicle of emanation of a powerful deity whose mission is to protect the Land of Snows, and also to help its light shine for the benefit of all beings.

It may be useful to point out a common error outside Tibet, which interprets the Gyalwa Rinpoche, the Precious Victorious One, as a kind of "god-king" in the eyes of his subjects. That very notion amuses Tibetans, because it represents such a misunderstanding of their worldview. For them, the Dalai Lama is a reincarnation of Chenresig, the Bodhisattva of Infinite Compassion. This divinity, also known as Avalokiteshvara in older Buddhist tradition, is a special protector of Tibet. Hence the Dalai Lama is both the personification of this protector, and at the same time an ordinary human being subject to the same laws as human beings in general: birth, aging, illness, and death. But the paradox is only one of appearance, for it is his status, qualities, and capacities which make him a very exceptional human being—but not a god.

The veneration which is showered upon him from his first recognition in infancy must not be confused with worship of the physical person. It is inspired by the spirit which is revealed through him, and which he incarnates: the very Buddha-nature itself. Of course the extravagance of devotion, sometimes resulting in a blind allegiance on the part of his subjects, can seem surprising or strange. Yet this crucial distinction remains very much in effect, and no one is more aware of this than the current Dalai Lama himself, as he has made clear on many occasions. His older brother, Thubten Jigme Norbu, is also quite lucid on this subject:

> We express gratitude to Chenresig for having entered into a human form in such a way as to show us more effectively the direction we need to take. [...] We Tibetans have never pretended to be better than others. On the contrary, we believe that Chenresig was sent to us because we were such a wild and barbaric people.[26]

Growing up at a distance from the rest of the world, if not completely sheltered from it, the young boy is prepared for his destiny. This may be considered as a continuity which is both eternal and changing, or as simply a new bodily envelope for an ancient consciousness. In any case, his fundamental training is a very rigorous one, as it is for all other high lamas who have chosen to return among their disciples. Yet it is especially the case for the one who symbolizes the very essence of Tibetan Buddhism, and bears both temporal and spiritual responsibilities for his people. Hope then lies in the operation of a subtle alchemy, in an apparently continuous current composed of a dual movement of energies from above to below (compassion) and from below to above (veneration).

Solid foundations are needed in order to meet the requirements of such high aims, and the current Dalai Lama's masters seem to have made every effort to provide them. This resulted in a young man who was certainly highly gifted, if not always very industrious,

---

[26] Thubten Jigme Norbu and Colin Turnbull, *Tibet, its History, Religion and People* (New York: Penguin, 1969).

and who quickly became the symbol of the rock upon which his people placed all their burdens, hopes, and dreams. Under the double supervision of Trijang Rinpoche and Ling Rinpoche, the tutors
who accompanied him from his infancy through his exile, until their
own deaths in Dharamsala in the early 1980s, Tenzin Gyatso was initiated at a very early age into the five major disciplines of the Tibetan
Buddhist education: Sanskrit, Tibetan culture and art, medicine,
logic, and philosophy.

The latter subject is subdivided into five branches, which are difficult even for adults: the Buddhist scripture known as the *Prajna-
Paramita,* or Perfection of Wisdom; the *Madhyamika,* or Middle Way;
the *Vinaya,* or monastic discipline; and the *Abidharma,* an ancient
doctrine of metaphysics. To this are added the *Pramana,* or five
minor ramifications, consisting of music, poetic style, dialectics, the-
ater, and astrology. A special value is accorded to dialectics, or the
art of debate. Surrounding this central curriculum are a myriad of
commentaries, explanations, and interpretations.

A prior foundation of these studies is provided by the texts of
the Kangyour and the Tanjour, which all ordained monks are supposed to know thoroughly, if not by heart. The first series includes
some 118 volumes, or 48,000 scriptures of the direct teachings of
Buddha and some of his closest disciples. The second is composed
of 225 volumes of commentaries edited over the centuries by scholarly Tibetan and Indian masters. The Four Great Tantras, which are
also referred to as the secret or hidden tradition, are included in
this series. But no one can begin to learn these without an adequate
preparation, ordinarily requiring (so it is said) some twenty years of
studies limited to the level of mere opinion.

At the solemn moment of entry into the monastic order, the
novice must perform a certain ritual which is the very cornerstone
of Buddhist engagement: the "taking of refuge." Here, one places
one's life and actions permanently under the omnipresent auspices
of the Three Jewels (or Triple Jewel): the Buddha, the Dharma (cos-
mic law or design), and the Sangha (spiritual community). This is

a founding practice and terminology common to virtually all forms of Buddhism the world over.

Tibetan Buddhists sometimes add a fourth aspect to this refuge, which is the spiritual teacher or lama regarded as one's living guru, transmitter of the teaching and initiation, and guide on the path of Awakening. The master is considered to incarnate the threefold essence of the faith: spirit, word, and body, called *sanggye, chös,* and *gendun* in Tibetan. However, we should bear in mind that each of these words has several possible interpretations, depending on the context, religious or secular, in which it appears. Also, there are multiple levels of meaning for each step of the path—from the most basic, or exoteric, to the most subtly esoteric. Furthermore, in Tibetan Buddhist tradition, the relationship between teacher and disciple imposes just as many obligations upon the latter as upon the former.

Such was the path upon which the young Tenzin Gyatso embarked, though at his age he could hardly have realized the full extent of such a commitment. Passing through degree after degree upon the way, he began to mount the endless steps towards a knowledge and wisdom which he now characterizes as an ongoing, daily learning process, not a fixed attainment. The educational demands made upon a Dalai or a Panchen Lama are of a rigor which reflects the strict verifications previously made in determining their reincarnational identity. Even though the Dalai Lama is regarded as the secular chief of his people, his religious role is more important, and it is this which dominates his education. In this sense his primary responsibility consists of a thorough study of the texts of Tsong-Khapa's reformist school known as "the practitioners of virtue." From a very early age, he is required to immerse himself in these texts.

Such knowledge must be renewed in each incarnation, for certain memories and knowledge fade away—according to Tibetan Buddhism, this normally applies to book-learning. However, the fruits of practice are considered to be transmissible from one life-time to another, and it is for this reason that practice is held in such high esteem, as the best basis of a safe-conduct through the gates of death, and also of an auspicious reconstruction of a new personality and embodiment. As for the studies themselves, it is considered best to conduct them as if it were for the first time, even though in some instances it may be clear that they are refreshments of previous memories.

> I am not concerned with what others think of me, whether they are my disciples or not. And even though some may consider me as omniscient, from my own point of view I am just a traveler on the way, and I have a long way to go. Of course I have the status of Dalai Lama, I am the Dalai Lama, but as an individual I am nothing more than a monk whose greatest desire is to learn more, to receive teachings and use them in a good way. In Tibetan Buddhism, the continuity of transmission lineages is of crucial importance. [...]
>
> In fact, this is not a matter of knowing or not knowing something. One must have received the continuity of the teaching, for we feel that without it the true blessing cannot be transmitted. Learning through reading or discussion is not the same thing. In order for the tradition to live, there must be initiation by a living master who is qualified and experienced. As for myself, I am confident that because I am the Dalai Lama, and have followed these teachings in other lives, I am able to instruct a person in the continuity of the tradition. But in order to do this, I myself had to receive the direct authority which can only be conferred by an authentic master.[27]

---

[27] Claude B. Levenson, *Le Seigneur du Lotus blanc* (Paris: Livre de Poche, 1989).

Tenzin Gyatso did not lack for such masters around him. With his openness and tolerance, he has practically never ceased to be a learner himself. He has especially studied the teachings of schools of Tibetan Buddhism which differ from his own, and has long sought contact and dialogue with completely different ways of seeing the world. During the time when he was a virtual recluse in the Potala and at Norbulingka, visitors were rare, yet typically asked for an audience with him. He readily accorded this, often because he learned much from quietly observing them. In any case, the strict rules of protocol then in effect did not favor verbal communications.

Separated early from his family, the Dalai Lama has lived virtually all his life as a monk. Even his brothers and sisters see him first and foremost as a spiritual teacher, and treat him with the same deference as do other Tibetans. Only with his mother did he have any real family intimacy, and this lasted through exile, to the very end of her life. He has a less vivid memory of his father, since he was only twelve when he died.

These years of his life, between winters at the Potala and summers at Norbulingka, were in general conducted as they had been for centuries. Yet this involved a complexity which stimulated plenty of curiosity in a child of his age. Although the two palaces were less than two miles apart, protocol demanded an interminably long process of moving from one to the other. The change of seasons was also accompanied by formal changes in administrative practices, and in official dress as well.

Finally the day arrived when the young sovereign was ceremoniously placed in his palanquin, and transported to the summer palace, with his subjects prostrating all along the way. He would have far preferred to cover this ground on horseback or on foot, so as to "enjoy at leisure the beauty of nature, with the soft green of new growth everywhere," which enchanted him. After a long and tedious ritual, the departure finally got underway, and the colorful procession tottered along, with its richly saddled horses, and its young Dalai

Lama sitting behind the drawn curtains of the palanquin, impatient to arrive at his destination.

The youth was always glad to leave the imposing fortress-palace with its thousand rooms for the summer dwelling, located at the center of a vast garden-park. Life was less austere there, and this palace seemed almost rustic by comparison. Although his discipline was not relaxed, the routine was more pleasant in this milder and more open environment. Animals wandered the lanes in semi-liberty, where musk deer rubbed shoulders with impressive mastiff watchdogs. Haughty Mongolian camels brought an air of the vast open steppes to these grounds, and there were also peacocks and cranes which enchanted him with their beauty. Two leopards and an old tiger in a cage inspired the child with his first reflections on the notion of freedom, which was unclear to him at that time. He nevertheless remembers being very unhappy upon learning that the wings of a flock of Canada geese had been trimmed so as to prevent them from flying.

By closely observing the behavior of these animals, and interacting with them over the years, the boy began to glean some impressions about the nature of the world and its creatures in general, including himself. Thus the little fish people who lived in the pond would generally come quickly when he arrived. He would often throw them bits of bread, and later tried to assure a fair distribution of this food among them with the aid of a little boat. Sometimes, though, the fish people would not show up. On such occasions he would try to attract their attention by throwing pebbles, but this only made them flee further, and put him in a bad mood as well. One day at the pond he tried to retrieve a floating stick, and fell in. Only the alertness of a passing janitor saved his life. He also loved to go with his younger brother for a ride inside a certain boat which had room only for the two of them, to the dismay of their servants, who had to follow the boat by walking along the banks.

Tenzin Gyatso also recalls some strong emotions associated with a certain parrot. There were many at Norbulingka, but this bird had become especially friendly with one of his three main servants, who often had treats for the bird to eat. The boy also wanted to be close to this bird, but the latter seemed quite indifferent to his advances. Vexed and frustrated by this rejection, he once seized a stick and tried to strike the recalcitrant bird. The latter quickly flew away, and thereafter totally avoided the child.

But in general the adult Dalai Lama remembers these years as full of happy and affectionate experiences with animals, as well as of the beauty of nature in general. He learned gardening there, which he still practices with pleasure at his residence at Dharamsala. For a time which was to be temporary, but was extended indefinitely, some Lhassan apsos (a Tibetan breed of miniature dog) lived with the family.

Later, when the conditions of his life changed so radically, and the Dalai Lama began to live in his own house, several cats came to enliven his solitude. He reflects on pets in general:

> ...no matter how tame and well-treated animals are, they always harbor some trace of a desire to escape. This has only reinforced my conviction that the desire for freedom is fundamental to all living beings.[28]

Like any monk, the Dalai Lama had to follow the classic sequence of his order. First his novitiate *(rabjung),* in which he took 16 fundamental vows; then the *getsul* period, in which 30 more are added; and before attaining the complete ordination, or *gelong,* he had to commit himself to a total of 253 vows. No doubt his own way of meeting these conditions was unusual, living as he did mostly in solitude, under the constant attention of his tutors and masters, who initiated

---

[28] Claude B. Levenson, *Le Seigneur du Lotus blanc* (Paris: Livre de Poche, 1989).

him in the subtleties of the teachings in such a way that his progress was far more rapid than that of an ordinary monk.

He remembers looking with envy upon other young monks of his age, who were allowed much more recreation time, playing and wrestling with each other in the courtyard, while he had to follow the strict discipline of his studies. However much he modestly admits to his laziness, his mentors were unanimous in considering his progress to be very rapid.

As the Dalai Lama's training continued, following the natural rhythms of the seasons and punctuated by ancient traditional ritu als, the flames of war and social upheaval continued to mount in the outside world. Entire countries were disappearing and being born in the wake of a crumbling colonialism, civil conflicts were being settled with modern arms, and regimes of power were rising and falling everywhere. In the immediate aftermath of the Second World War, India finally achieved its emancipation from Great Britain. In China, Mao Tse-tung and his armies were defeating Chiang Kai-shek, and the Berlin-Rome-Tokyo axis was crumbling, as Stalin and Roosevelt prepared to meet at Yalta and divide the spoils of a devastated Europe.

The echoes of these momentous events always seemed to reach Lhassa in an attenuated form. The regency power of those years never seemed to grasp the urgency, nor even the relevancy, of the repercussions of these events for their own immediate future. Even when the cards had already been dealt and played, their faces seemed indecipherable by the rulers of a society steeped in its own traditions, and long isolated from developments in the outside world.

The Dalai Lama remembers the end of the hostilities, formally announced when he was ten years old. It was up to the regent, in consensus with the *kashag*, to make the appropriate state decisions. That year of 1945 also saw other events which were minor in comparison, yet full of significance for Tibet in these changing times. By intermediary of the British mission at Lhassa, Richard Parker arrived from England charged with the task of teaching English in a school opened by his government especially for that purpose. A few months later, protests from the heads of the major monasteries forced its closure. This was also the year when two Austrians, Heinrich Harrer and Peter Aufschnaiter, fleeing a prisoner-of-war camp at Dehra Dun in the Indian Himalayas, sought refuge in Lhassa. They remained there for seven years, and built up an excellent rapport with the local population and authorities. Harrer was even granted access to the Potala, and had several friendly meetings with the young Dalai Lama, to whom he taught the rudiments of English, as well as giving him information about the outside world.

Yet none of this had any effect on the stark reality of Mao's growing power. His forces were already in position, whether intentionally or not at this point, to prepare the trap which would not be long in closing upon Tibet. So it was that a certain Geshe Sherab Gyatso, a scholar of Drepung monastery whose pro-Chinese sympathies were known, had already secured a place for himself on the Commission for Mongolian and Tibetan Affairs. Desiring to return to his monastery at Lhassa after a long period of study in China, he was denied permission to enter when he arrived at Nagchuka. The Tibetan authorities suspected him of planning to disseminate communist propaganda in the monasteries. Some years later he would take his revenge, as he re-entered Tibet riding in the Jeeps of the conquering Chinese army.

Also in 1945, an official delegation was dispatched from Lhassa to the British authorities in India, bearing gifts and messages of congratulations to the victors of W.W.II. The emissaries, who were traveling with Tibetan passports, were received in New Delhi both by Lord Wavell, the Viceroy, and by the U.S. ambassador to India. Hugh Richardson, chief of the British mission at Lhassa, had previously warned the Tibetans that his government might have to participate in discussions with the Chinese national assembly in Peking, who were claiming that such official action on the part of Tibet, implying that it was a sovereign nation, was in violation of the Simla accords of 1914.

In spite of this warning, and in spite of Tibetan assurances to the British of their own restraint in this matter, when the delegation returned from India (passing through a part of China as they had to do in those days) they made a detour to Peking to attend this assembly. Why? Even today, no one is sure to what extent it was due to deliberate disobedience, to misunderstanding, to clever manipulation, or to simple curiosity. In any case, the Tibetan delegation found themselves sitting in the great hall of the Chinese deputies. The Tibetan version of this event remains today that they went there only as "observers." The Chinese, on the other hand, declared that their very presence there was an official act of allegiance to China (although just in case they hadn't made it, the Chinese had previously procured their own "Tibetan" delegation, who were also in attendance). Whatever the truth of all this, the Dalai Lama was still too young to take an active hand in this affair.

Although the true nature of this event was never clear, it nevertheless served as a pretext a few years later for pushing through the notorious "Seventeen Point Agreement," which Peking was to adopt as its primary justification for taking over Tibet. According to the Tibetan version of things, the very presence of the official Tibetan delegation at the Pan-Asiatic Conference in New Delhi in 1947 proves that Tibet was already acting as an independent and sovereign nation. Their national flag flew as an equal alongside those of the other nations at that conference.

Even while events threatened Tibet from the outside, things within the country were not going so well either. More serious than the monks' reactionary expulsion of the English school was their opposition, alongside that of privileged landowners and bureaucrats, to the governmental decision in 1944 which forgave all payments of interest (which had sometimes been accumulating for years and even generations) on loans made to the poorest farmers by wealthy monasteries and other privileged classes. In the district of Lhundup Dzong, farmers promptly stopped making back payments to the schools of Sera Je and Ngagpa, and were supported in this by the district chief. The dispute grew more and more bitter, finally erupting into violence when some monks abducted the official and beat him to death. This scandal reached the headquarters of the monastery near Lhassa, yet its authorities refused to bring the guilty parties to justice by turning them over to an official investigative commission. And as a reprisal for the non-payment of interest, the monks of the two schools refused to participate in the festivities for the Great Prayer in 1945. This in turn led to law officials being sent to the monastery to arrest the ringleaders, and at the same time divesting the abbots of the two schools of their functions.

To add to this strife, a bitter quarrel erupted between ex-regent Reting Rinpoche and the current regent, Taktra Rinpoche. This fueled fears and rumors regarding a personal rivalry between the two lamas. Some claimed that there had long been a secret agreement for the two men to alternate as regent, and that Taktra Rinpoche was not honoring this agreement, thus provoking Reting Rinpoche's resentment.

Some months later this climate was further inflamed by an abortive ambush attempt against the son of a high official involved in the matter, and by a booby-trapped package sent to the regent. A coded message, warning that the ex-regent had sent a secret message to Chiang Kai-shek denouncing the current regent, was the spark which set off the gunpowder. Soldiers were sent to Reting monastery, with orders to bring the ex-regent to Lhassa. On the day of his arrival there, a plot to rescue him on the part of the monks of Sera was foiled, he and his entourage were placed under house arrest, and an investigation was begun.

The result of a close examination of the papers and correspondence of the old monk showed that it was his close aides and colleagues who had engineered all these incidents, from which Reting

Rinpoche himself had kept aloof, vainly exhorting his associates to refrain from violent actions. Nevertheless, he was judged to be implicated in a conspiracy to unseat the current regent, and his request for a personal audience with the Dalai Lama was denied, without even consulting the youth. Investigations were still going on, when his sudden death in 1947 added still more to the atmosphere of confusion.

The Dalai Lama himself was privy to only a few repercussions of these events:

> One day when I was listening to a debate, I heard sounds of gunfire. They came from the north, from the direction of the Sera monastery. I ran quickly outside, excited at the idea that my telescope would be of real use at last. But I was also troubled by the thought that these sounds I was hearing meant death for someone. Finally, it was said that Reting Rinpoche, who had announced his retirement six years ago, had now taken it into his head to reclaim the regency. [...] Since I was still a minor, it was natural for my advisors to try to protect me from these problems, but when I reflect more deeply on this, I wonder if I might not have been able to do something useful in this case.[29]

For the time being, his studies would remain paramount in his life, week after week, month after month. There were some intervals of leisure, notably on days of the full moon, and the long-anticipated reunions with his family. On these days he was allowed to spend a few hours with brothers, sisters, and cousins in the large family house not far from the Potala. Yet even this was not true freedom, nor even a time of full relaxation. The reverent distance because of his status as divine incarnation remained in effect, a virtually automatic response on the part of the family and household.

---

[29] Claude B. Levenson, *Le Seigneur du Lotus blanc* (Paris: Livre de Poche, 1989).

Even when I was quite young, I abhorred ceremony and etiquette, much preferring the company of servants to that of government officials. I especially liked my parents' servants. Most of them came from Amdo province, and I loved hearing them speak of my native village and surrounding country.[30]

Yet such interludes were relatively brief, and came to an end when the Dalai Lama reached the age of twelve, marking the end of an important cycle in this human life. He was already preparing for his first tests as dialectician, before a public assembly of monks and abbots from the three schools of Drepung and the two schools of Sera. A challenge for any monk, it was an intimidating prospect for this twelve-year-old boy, in spite of the reverence which was accorded him in the austerity and quasi-solitude of his apartments in the heights of the Potala.

Tenzin Gyatso feels that the apprehension he felt during these debates was due to finding himself "for the first time in this life" in front of those venerable old walls which "appeared almost familiar to me. And it soon seemed clear to me that I did know them from previous lives."

It was also during this period that the regent transmitted the special teaching of the fifth Dalai Lama to him. Revealed in a vision, this teaching has never been known outside a very small number who are considered able to understand it. It also contains instructions which are reserved exclusively for the personal practice of the Tibetan sovereign. After receiving this initiation, the Dalai Lama says that he began to have unusual experiences in the form of dreams.

Some strange outer phenomena occurred with a surprising regularity during this period, when the conflict between nationalists and communists in China was mounting in intensity. These phenomena were considered disturbing, yet difficult to explain or

---

[30] Claude B. Levenson, *Le Seigneur du Lotus blanc* (Paris: Livre de Poche, 1989).

interpret. In the middle of the dry season, when not the slightest cloud was to be seen in the sky, on the roof of the Jokhang in the heart of Lhassa, a gold-painted gargoyle began to discharge water in a continuous and disagreeable trickle, which was unheard-of in this season. At the same time, for several weeks a bright light resembling that of a comet illuminated the sky, causing fear. A few old Lhassans remembered a similar phenomenon, seen in 1910, just before a Chinese invasion...

There were also rumors of monstrous births; and the sudden collapse of an ancient stone pillar erected at the foot of the Potala in the year 763 C.E. added to the general feeling of malaise. In July, 1949, the Tibetan government expelled the Chinese mission from Lhassa, fed up with Peking's manipulations regarding the succession of the Panchen Lama. The diplomats and their families were very politely accompanied to the border, but with armed escort, and with an injunction not to return.

In the autumn of that year, after the defeat of the nationalist armies, and very soon after taking over power in Peking, the communist regime broadcast its intention of "liberating" Tibet over national radio. Astounded by this declaration, the Tibetans could not believe their ears, and tried naively to comfort themselves with the conclusion that this proposal was so crazy that it simply was not to be taken seriously. Several months later, in the summer of the following year, an unexpected, terrifying event was interpreted as a warning, yet the precise meaning of it was not understood at the time. It would not be long, however, before the worst fears would be confirmed.

It was a beautiful summer evening just before the opening of the opera season at Lhassa. Normally, theatrical performances and games of skill filled this week of festivities, and there were singers, poets, jugglers, wrestlers and acrobats everywhere, surrounded by joyous and enthusiastic crowds of Tibetans dressed in their finest. There was even a hotly contested flower competition, attended by ladies from the highest social classes, and rivaling each other in their luxurious jewelry and attire. Officials appeared in their ceremonial clothes for the occasion, and everyone else wore costumes inspired by the moment. But in that year of 1950, nature herself chose to intervene in a dramatic way, as if to warn against such an excessively carefree atmosphere.

In mid-August, a very violent earthquake shook the high plains of Tibet near Chamdo, and the shocks were felt in Lhassa, in Sakya, and as far away as Calcutta. For hours the skies were lit up with flaming displays, filled with a blood-colored light, and with strange patterns of bright stripes. Sinister crackling noises filled the air, and violent explosions were heard. Later, it was learned that hundreds of small villages had disappeared, that entire valleys had been opened by displaced mountains, and that the Yarlung Tsangpo river, more famously known downstream as the Brahmaputra, had changed its course. For eyewitness Robert Ford, a British radio technician who was working for the Tibetan government at Chamdo, "This was no ordinary earthquake. It felt like the end of the world." And in a sense, it was.

In the Heart of Danger

Whether ordinary earthquake or evil portent, this event of August, 1950 deeply affected Tibetans. Those who were there still remember it vividly, and it has become inscribed in the collective memory as a major historical event, recounted as such to new generations. Even the traditional joyousness of the opera season at Lhassa was rather dampened by it, and the festival atmosphere was infected by a subtle underlying disquiet, although the colorful spectacles were all performed as usual.

Another incident came to trouble the atmosphere on the third day of the festival, when a messenger arrived at nightfall, and was immediately sent to see the regent. His arrival was little-noticed, but did not escape the attention of the young Dalai Lama, who happened to be watching from the space reserved for officials. Still too young to be regularly consulted on all decisions, he could not find an acceptable way to inquire about this event. Yet his curiosity won out, and he climbed a ladder which led to a window in his private apartment, where he could listen and watch Taktra Rinpoche in the next room without being seen. The latter grew more and more grim as the message was read, and instead of returning to his place at the festivities, the regent immediately ordered a meeting of the *kashag*, the cabinet of ministers.

A little later, the Dalai Lama was informed of a telegram from the governor of Kham province, announcing an attack by Chinese soldiers upon a Tibetan outpost, causing the death of the local military commander. Other armed skirmishes had occurred in this region in previous months. Now it seemed that the Chinese intention to "liberate" Tibet was not just mad raving, but a serious threat. This new provocation was clearly a prelude to invasion, and the Tibetan army was totally unprepared for it, having so long been despised and neglected because of traditional attitudes towards professional soldiers.

In the ensuing battles, outnumbered and poorly-equipped Tibetan soldiers showed great heroism, and often foiled their enemies with clever and devastating warrior's ruses. Yet there were also retreats, and even treachery. The key to this overall failure, according to the Dalai Lama, may be found in fundamental Tibetan attitudes: "In spite of their history, Tibetans are fundamentally peaceful. For them, the worst possible profession is that of the military—in their eyes, soldiers are just butchers."

To make matters even more hopeless, the army's equipment consisted mostly of outdated rifles, a few old cannons, and no military vehicles. On the other hand, Tibetans are unsurpassed in fighting on horseback, and in their hands the slingshot becomes a very deadly weapon. But what can even hordes of such skillful warriors accomplish in immense plains filled with a vast, ant-like army whose commanders, trained by a cold and calculating logic of numbers, care little about the lives lost among their own troops, as long as they win? Furthermore, the overwhelming recent victory over the nationalist Chinese had left Mao's armies in an enthusiastic and bellicose mood, hypnotized by revolutionary propaganda, and ready to carry out his will whatever the cost.

In spite of these events, life at Lhassa seemed to return to its habitual rhythms after the opera season, with the Dalai Lama plunged once more in his studies, and his advisors torn between their obligation to assure his education and the ever more urgent need to prepare him for the delicate and complex affairs of state which awaited him.

In hopes of clarifying the situation with China, two delegates were dispatched to Peking. At that period, the easiest route was through

The Dalai Lama at sixteen, during a theological examination.

India to Hong Kong. While awaiting visas in New Delhi, they were told to remain there in order to meet first with the new Chinese ambassador to India, who would soon arrive to take up his post.

Meanwhile they met in India with Jawaharlal Nehru, and discussed the necessity of an official status of neutrality for Tibet, as an independent buffer-state between the two Asian giants. Nehru offered opinions, but refused to commit himself to anything. The ambassador, Yan Chung-hsien, finally arrived late at the discussion, immediately imposing certain conditions: that Tibet be recognized as an integral part of China, and that it turn over its military forces to the latter. Only after accepting these conditions would the Tibetans be allowed to travel to Peking so as to formalize an accord. The delegates of course refused, keeping in touch with Lhassa as discussions continued. The ambassador went through the motions of listening to the latter, yet for Peking the decision had already been made.

The situation worsened later in the autumn, when two military columns crossed over the Dri-chu, east of the small town of Chamdo. It cost many lives for the Chinese army, in spite of the apparent restraint now being exercised by the authorities in Peking. Besides the many heroic acts of Tibetan resistance to the human steamroller, the Chinese also lost many men because of bad supplies, and the harsh mountain weather, for which they were unprepared. All the roads which lead from the Chinese plains to the Land of Snows are difficult, and paved with the bones of centuries of such human sacrifice. Yet this time the numbers were to prove too great, and even the tenacity and bravery of the Tibetan defenders could not make up for the lack of any real outside support. The world seemed indifferent, or tepid at best, to the fate of Tibet, and this only encouraged the Chinese regime in its aggression.

With the reluctant support of Great Britain, India nevertheless formally protested to Peking. The suave response was an attempt to soothe the Indians by assuring them that China's own interests dictated extreme prudence in this matter, and Nehru seemed convinced of the good faith of the new masters of the Forbidden City, and of their intention to respect previous agreements. In November, 1950, the Tibetan cabinet appealed to the United Nations, but were snubbed, not even receiving a reply to two telegrams. At last the Tibetans began to understand the enormity of the cost of their international isolation, and especially of the isolationism imposed by a conservative ideology. The land of lamas, magic, and mystery was finding itself ever more alone and abandoned to its fate.

In Lhassa, the authorities were in confusion as to what policy to adopt. In spite of growing fear among the people, lively satirical verses and songs began to appear, mercilessly criticizing the indecision and incompetence of the government. This criticism soon grew more vehement, and tracts and posters appeared demanding that the Dalai Lama be given his full governing powers. But he was still only sixteen, and tradition specified that he be at least eighteen before his education could be considered sufficient to assume these responsibilities. Nevertheless, the corridors of power reverberated with strong disagreement about this, for many officials held with the popular opinion that the current extraordinary circumstances demanded they make an exception.

Thus it was decided to consult the Nechung oracle, by whose human medium Dorje Drakden is supposed to speak—one of the most powerful and awesome divine protectors of the country, whose counsel no one can afford to ignore. As usual, the consultation was prepared with all the care required by the ceremony. The Dalai Lama clearly remembers the palpable tension in the shrine room filled with incense, and with a silence as oppressive as the hundred-pound ritual costume worn by the medium.

However, on this occasion things went unusually quickly. As if propelled by an external force, the man in deep trance hurtled towards the adolescent, prostrating himself in front of him, in spite of the weight of his helmet. He placed a *khata* scarf upon the youth's knees and exclaimed: "The time has come. Make him king!" Then he fainted into unconsciousness, and was quickly taken away by special servants, whose job was to undress him and very carefully help him to return to normal consciousness.

After such an unequivocal result, it only remained to obey the oracle and begin preparations for the official enthronement ceremony. Taktra Rinpoche immediately offered his resignation as regent, though he remained as chief advisor to the Dalai Lama. Astrologers were consulted as to the most propitious date, which was fixed as the seventeenth of November, 1950. Although no doubts were any longer to be heard about this, the Dalai Lama himself admits that he had some. The prospect of taking on the leadership of a country threatened by war, and upsetting his whole routine of life, consisting mostly of studies and training, had catapulted him into an unknown reality.

> This challenge filled me with anxiety. I was not quite sixteen years old, and far from completing my religious training. I knew nothing of the outside world, and had no political experience. Yet I was sufficiently mature to be aware of my own ignorance, and of how much I needed to learn. In my role as Dalai Lama, I was the only person whom everyone in the country would follow without dissent. Yet I felt hesitant. The national assembly met and formally presented the request to the cabinet. Then, fully realizing the gravity of the situation, I saw that I could no longer indulge in avoiding my responsibilities. I had to assume them, had to leave my adolescence behind and prepare myself as best I could to lead the country, in the face of the enormous power of communist China. Thus I accepted, though not without some apprehension.[31]

On this eleventh day of the tenth month of the year of the Iron Tiger, the ceremonies were lavish, and there was great rejoicing. A general amnesty was proclaimed, and even the threat surrounding

---

[31] Claude B. Levenson, *Le Seigneur du Lotus blanc* (Paris: Livre de Poche, 1989).

the country seemed to subside for awhile. Even though miracles would not arrive to save the Country of the Gods from the harsh realities of this human world, the Tibetans joined in a joyous communion of celebration of the return of their sovereign in his full role.

Well before the formal investiture, Tenzin Gyatso was all too aware of what awaited him. Two weeks previously, his older brother Thubten Jigme Norbu, *tulku* of Taktser and abbot of Kumbum monastery, had arrived at Lhassa. He bore bad news, surpassing their worst fears and confirming the rumors of atrocities recently brought to the capital by travelers and refugees. He himself had seen the arrival of the vanguard of the Chinese troops, and was for a time essentially held prisoner in his monastery.

Making the monks their special targets, the Chinese commanders did not hesitate to inflict torture even upon old lamas. Their arrogance and hatred contrasted bizarrely with their promises of a radiant future, and even the humblest and poorest monks were outraged at the Chinese treatment of their superiors. General popular resentment was also increased by the invaders' demand to be fed by the Tibetans, which created shortages and inflation.

More surprising for the young Dalai Lama, and appalling to a Buddhist monk, the Chinese officials not only acted as if the country were already conquered, they openly sought to corrupt his brother. Using promises and threats, they sent him on to Lhassa so as to win over his younger brother to their cause. If the older brother succeeded in this, they promised to reward him richly. If he failed, they gave him permission to kill the Dalai Lama and take his place. Wisely concealing his shock at this obscene proposition, Thubten Jigme Norbu played along with the Chinese and pretended to be going to Lhassa to accomplish this plan, so as not to arouse suspicions.

A year of Chinese military presence had made the real intentions of the invaders clear to Norbu. He had long reflected on the consequences of this occupation, and now shared these with his brother.

Norbu's plan was to leave behind his monk's clothes and his country, and travel abroad, seeking foreign military aid with the utmost urgency. In his eyes, an effective armed resistance was the only solution for Tibet, and help was needed for this.

But the Dalai Lama did not share this view. At that time, he still held firmly to the principles of non-violence founded on the teaching of the Buddha. Admitting that certain specific situations do require actions which are outwardly violent, he nevertheless remained convinced that "Everything ultimately turns out for the best." Such was the way he had chosen by deep conviction, and he never wavered from it, in spite of the intransigence of his adversary. Even today, he tirelessly maintains that only the power of negotiation can enable his people to survive, and the refugees to finally return home.

However, shortly after the investiture ceremony, in which he was given the Golden Wheel, symbol of his temporal power, the Dalai Lama accepted the counsel of his closest advisors, and made plans to withdraw temporarily from Lhassa. A retreat space was being prepared for him at the Dromo/Tatung monastery, not far from the Sikkim border. All precautions were being taken so as to be ready for the worst—Chinese repression had not abated, and some feared for the personal safety of the Dalai Lama.

Tenzin Gyatso's debut as head of state was anything but easy. Certain traditional protocols were completely irrelevant to the urgency of the situation, and he foresaw the need for fundamental reforms in order to adapt to the new times. He barely had time to think about it, but he nevertheless reflected on these things. Hampered by administrational mechanisms of excessive complexity, relics of an ancient and slower pace of life, he went along with the custom and named two prime ministers: Lobsang Tashi, a monk, and Lukhangwa, a citizen of high reputation. Given the place of religion in Tibetan society, responsibility tended to be divided between monastic and secular at every hierarchical level. Yet the general tendency was for monastic officials to abandon responsibility for practical applications to their civil colleagues. This sometimes resulted in abuses and litigation, and did much to justify the image of backwardness and injustice associated with Tibetan social power in the past.

While preparations continued for his voyage south, the Dalai Lama did his best to manage his routine, and even to find some time to continue his studies while he could—it was as if he foresaw that times were coming when far more demanding tasks would leave no space at all for studies. Not without humor, he admits that it was just at that time that he suddenly discovered a newfound passion for study, and an understanding of its primary value in forming a balanced personality.

Everything was finally ready by the end of the year. Several caravans had already left discreetly, since the Dalai Lama's impending departure was a secret. Curious by nature, the adolescent rejoiced at the prospect of being able to escape for awhile from the boredom of protocol and the routine which imprisoned him. He was all the more pleased at the plan for him to travel incognito—certainly with a competent escort, but without any of the luxury and pomp which normally accompanied his every move. The trip would take about ten days.

The caravan got moving during the night, leaving the Potala with the measured rhythms of the horses and pack animals.

> It was cold, but the sky was clear. In Tibet, the stars have a brightness I've never seen anywhere else. We made our way in silence. The least whinnying of a horse startled me, but I wasn't really afraid.[32]

Did he already sense that this departure in civil disguise was a forerunner for another one some years later, one which would close

---

[32] Claude B. Levenson, *Le Seigneur du Lotus blanc* (Paris: Livre de Poche, 1989).

the doors of his country to him, and open the doors of the world? To this question, the Dalai Lama answers only with a silent smile.

But in spite of all the precautions, the importance of this caravan did not go unnoticed. There were a number of high lamas and officials in it who were all too recognizable. Soon a crowd of thousands of monks from the "Three Pillars of Tibet"—the Sera, Drepung, and Ganden monasteries—who were gathered not far from Lhassa for their traditional winter debates, spotted Ling Rinpoche in the caravan, one of the two tutors of the Dalai Lama. Approaching him, they begged him not to allow their Precious Protector to leave. The young Dalai Lama was deeply moved by this display of confidence in him, whereas he himself still wondered at his ability to meet the challenges facing him.

For him, this was a voyage full of learning. He was well aware that this was a rare opportunity to observe the conditions of life of his subjects at close hand, and at every stop he asked questions, trying to learn of hardships in the people's lives, or simply chatting uninhibitedly with anyone he had a chance to meet. Listening deeply to others, he learned more on this trip about his country and the lives of its people than in all the official reports he had read.

A week after their departure, the secret had completely leaked out, and when they arrived at Gyantse, fourth-largest town in the country, the atmosphere was almost solemn—hundreds of Tibetans had gathered along their path to greet their spiritual and now temporal sovereign. They were far more numerous in approaching him now, for this might be a unique chance to receive a personal blessing from him, which they would remember all their lives. However, they endeavored to keep this halt as short as possible, for everyone wanted to get to Dromo/Yatung and be able to rest a bit.

The caravan arrived there in January, 1951, after two weeks of slow going, yet without major difficulties. Everyone settled as best they could in this small town overwhelmed by the unprecedented presence of so many high dignitaries. These officials and their entourages were lodged in both official buildings and in private houses, whereas the Dalai Lama was welcomed to a peaceful accommodation at the small monastery of Dungkhar, perched on the edge of a hill overlooking the city. His two mentors, Ling Rinpoche and Trijang Rinpoche, accompanied him. His older brother, Taktser Rinpoche, also spent some last weeks with him before leaving for India and afterwards, the United States.

A Singhalese bonze came to visit, presenting a relic of the Buddha, which was interpreted as a very good omen. Thousands of the faithful from around the region, even from Sikkim, Bhutan, and India, gathered around him and took part in the ceremony organized for the occasion.

Other news was not so encouraging. Tibetan emissaries who had gone abroad in search of foreign support had found doors closed to them in the U.S., in Britain, in India, and in Nepal. Only the mission sent to Peking had been officially received—to learn that they had the right to listen and to keep their mouths shut. For the young Dalai Lama, the disappointment was deep, and cast doubt upon his previous trust in the ethical integrity of the leaders of these countries, as well as in their ability to respect their previous engagements.

Meanwhile Ngabo Ngawang Jigme, the governor of Chamdo province, gave him a lengthy report on the situation there, detailing the extent of the Chinese threat. He asked for authorization to go personally to Peking to negotiate. After consultation with his two main ministers who had remained in Lhassa, the Dalai Lama accepted this proposition, and sent four high officials to accompany the governor, two from Lhassa and two from Dromo.

But it turned out to be a Chinese trap. There were no negotiations, and the Tibetan envoys were put under house arrest and coerced into "signing" the infamous Seventeen Point Agreement, which essentially gives China permission to occupy Tibet. Forbidden to communicate with the Dalai Lama or anyone else in Lhassa, their signatures, even if authentic, would have been illegal and nonbinding, because unauthorized. But it is doubtful that all of them were even real. In any case, it has been definitely established that the "authentication" seals on the signatures are fakes, hastily manufactured in Peking, whereas the original seals had never left the possession of the Dalai Lama at his retreat in Yatung.

Yet this fraud succeeded in deceiving international authorities, even as impotent rage at the deception grew among the people of Tibet. The evil deed was done, and the Dalai Lama himself learned of it on the Tibetan language news broadcast of Chinese national radio on May 23, 1951, the very date of the "official" signature. He could scarcely believe his ears. Yet the tone of the announcer indicated that the manipulation was in deadly earnest. He knew that the trials that were in store for Tibet would be difficult indeed.

The very terms of the document are a rewriting of history to conform with the Chinese point of view. Contrary to this version, Tibetans have always known and proclaimed themselves to be a separate country—sharing a large border with China, certainly, and experiencing occasional territorial disputes with the latter, but entirely distinct in language, culture, religion, and ethnicity. But the Chinese international propaganda machine had gone into high gear, and Tibet had not the means to counter this barrage, especially when international leaders at that time were all too ready to sacrifice Tibet in a cowardly and expedient endorsement of Chinese pretensions. Shortly afterward, a telegram informed the Dalai Lama of the impending arrival in Yatung of the new governor of Tibet, Chang Chin-wu.

He had already been very busy trying to reconcile the contradictory opinions of his advisors as to what policy to adopt. His brother Taktser Rinpoche wrote from Calcutta, strongly encouraging him to take temporary refuge in India before it was too late, while seeking the U.S. support for which his brother had high hopes. This was also the prevailing opinion in the rest of his family, and Heinrich Harrer sent a message with similar advice from Kalimpong in Bhutan. On the other hand, his two leading ministers and the heads of the three great monasteries were urging him to return as soon as possible to Lhassa, where the people were showing signs of unrest. Ling Rinpoche also supported this point of view.

It was a serious dilemma for the teenage head of state, whose greatest strength lay in deep meditation, and whose main resource was prayer. Ignorant though he was of politics, he saw clearly that Washington was many thousands of miles away, and had no obvious interest in sending soldiers or military aid to defend Tibet; whereas neighboring China, with its hundreds of millions of people to feed, had plenty of reason to want to capture the Roof of the World and appropriate its wealth.

Perhaps hindsight shows that he underestimated the treachery of which his adversary was capable, but at that time the noble optimism of the young Dalai Lama, and his faith in the essential goodness of human nature held sway: he decided not to flee, and to remain among his people. He made use of the delay of the Chinese general's arrival by redoubling his efforts in his studies, including certain deeper teachings given to him by ex-regent Taktra Rinpoche. And he was finally free to walk and explore his surroundings, where the beauty of nature is a balm to the soul.

In mid-July an advance messenger arrived at Dungkhar monastery in the village of Dromo to inform the Dalai Lama of the arrival of the Chinese delegation. Tenzin Gyatso felt some nervousness on this occasion, and asked what was going to happen. "It was almost as if I were expecting to meet men with horns," he recalls. Immediately after this, he was standing on his roof when he caught sight of the dust of the approaching delegation along the road. As they drew closer, he saw the bright and lively colors of the traditional clothes of the Tibetan members of the party, alongside the dull grey colors of the Chinese trio—clothes as drab as the surface of the road they were walking on. This contrast was significant to him, symbolic of the shocks, both cultural and political, which were to come.

The first encounter between the young sovereign and the new commissar of Tibetan military and civil affairs was a foreshadowing, which has never been forgotten, of the bad times to come. The stony, flagrantly arrogant, and disrespectful attitude of the Chinese general puzzled the Dalai Lama. Yet he did not allow himself to become flustered by it. His own replies were circumspect, avoiding any pitfalls, and this gave him time to observe and take the measure of his adversary. The man's gold watch did not escape his keen regard, and when reflecting on this, he concluded that human beings were indeed similar in many ways, whatever their ideology or culture. He says that this taught him a lesson he did not forget.

Clearly anxious to maintain appearances of legality, General Chang Chin-wu first presented to the Dalai Lama a copy of the Seventeen Point Agreement detailing measures to be taken for the "peaceful liberation of Tibet." There were two amendments: the first regarding the future of the Tibetan army, and the second regarding the conditions of any future travel abroad by the Dalai Lama. He then demanded to know the latter's immediate plans, and when he intended to return to Lhassa. The Dalai Lama would say no more than "soon," perceiving that the Chinese official was impatient for him to return there—preferably immediately, and accompanied by the general—something which the Dalai Lama was quite determined to avoid.

The day following this frosty initial meeting, preparations nonetheless began for his return, this time more efficiently than when leaving Lhassa. At the beginning of August, the official caravan took the road back, but deliberately moved at a very leisurely pace. Now the Dalai Lama knew more about what he had to deal with, and he was determined to make the fullest use of all the limited—and closely watched—space of freedom that was left to him. Hence he took his time, stopping at every town and even in tiny hamlets, both to satisfy his own intense curiosity about his people and their living conditions, and to convey calm and encouragement by his example.

He also sought to reassure people—probably without being entirely convinced of it himself—that in spite of the foreign invasion of their country, the Chinese maintained that they came as friends. They even promised to leave Tibet, after their "brotherly assistance" had borne its fruit, enabling the Tibetans to achieve a better way of life. To further inspire his subjects, he gave brief public commentaries on religious texts, a new venture for him. According to those who were present, he did quite well at this. He also held audiences with local officials, village chiefs, and with common people. These meetings helped him to get a more intimate grasp of the situation in the field. He also heard grievances and demands which he planned to remedy by reforms to be undertaken as soon as feasible.

These varied activities while on the road filled his time, yet did not prevent him from somber reflections on the future, which he knew was going to be a deeply troubled one. He also took stock of his own profound commitment to his people, moved by their utter trust and devotion to him, which was demonstrated wherever he appeared. At times he was somewhat frightened by this awesome responsibility, for he felt not fully prepared for it. Nonetheless, he accepted it, telling himself that he had already made his choice long ago. How many thousands of times, and in how many previous lives, had he repeated the verses of the Bodhisattva Vow, which had been a part of his daily practice since childhood:

> As long as space exists
> As long as there are sentient beings
> May I also continue to live
> So as to dispel the sufferings of the world.

The return voyage to Lhassa was also an opportunity to marvel at the magnificent landscapes he encountered. He drank these in at leisure while riding a worthy old mule which had previously belonged to Reting Rinpoche. The caravan halted for several days at Gyantse, before rounding the Lake of Turquoise, the Yamdrock Tso, so as to reach the monastery of Samding. There were thousands of sheep grazing upon the great plains and hills, and to his joy they were accompanied by herds of wild deer and gazelles. He allowed himself to be enchanted by the brilliant summer light, savoring precious moments which are still engraved in his memory. Today he speaks of this time with a singular softness in his voice, indicating the power of those moments, as if he were nourishing himself from secret springs and forces of his native earth. From his stay at Samding, he cherishes the memory of a monastic community led for generations by the reincarnation of a feminine divinity, Dorje Phagmo, whose young abbess came to pay homage to him.

Before reaching Lhassa, the Dalai Lama took yet another detour so as to accompany Taktra Rinpoche to his monastery some hours from the capital. He spent several peaceful days there, taking counsel from the aged scholar, with whom this was to be his last meeting. When the time came for them to take leave of each other, the ex-regent asked the young sovereign to forgive him if he had sometimes been too strict with him when he was a child. The Dalai Lama was very touched by this, interpreting it as an excellent lesson in humility, exemplified by a true sage.

The return to Norbulingka in mid-August marked the return of his life to a familiar routine, or almost. The welcome home had been a fervent one, and the people seemed relieved to have the Dalai Lama back among them after an absence of nine months. The adolescent had deeply matured through his trials, and the awareness of his responsibility to save what could be saved. It would be years before he would begin to understand that his true personal destiny was to be one of exile, and of the experience of a new kind of freedom.

A Year in China

During his retreat at Yatung (had this been a foretaste of exile?) many things had changed in Lhassa. Tenzin Gyatso realized this immediately upon learning of the death of one of his closest youthful playmates, a janitor with an especially affectionate devotion to him. This felt to him like the closing of one of the last doors to his childhood. Although his solitude must have felt heavier because of this, he says, "My education taught me that it is vain to indulge in lamentation."

He now had to take up his difficult tasks as head of state, in addition to continuing his studies. In the beginning, his two chief ministers were able to protect him somewhat, but the screen was a thin one. He could not avoid having to deal directly with Chinese delegates, which was not a task he enjoyed.

Relations with the Chinese governor of Tibet were not improving. General Chang disliked being treated as a foreigner, if not a foreign invader. He had not taken kindly to being thwarted in his attempt to make his official entry into Lhassa at the side of the Dalai Lama. Also, during their first official meeting in Lhassa, when he was received according to tradition at the headquarters of the sovereign's personal guard, he lost his temper openly. "I was almost afraid, seeing him in such a state—his face quite red, his eyes bulging, sputtering so much that he seemed he might strangle, and pounding his fist on the table. But I discovered later that he was a man who got carried away too easily, yet also had a good-natured side."

But his arrogant and hostile attitude soon rendered the new governor odious to the Tibetan officials who had to work closely with him. This alienated them, and led to an insidious poisoning of the general atmosphere. In spite of his youth, the Dalai Lama quickly perceived this state of affairs. Yet he was unable to do much to improve things, for the underlying basis of relations with the governor seemed to amount to no more than the crude law of confrontation and threat of superior force.

For awhile the Tibetans held themselves in check, so as not to go against the will of the Dalai Lama, as they and the governor got to know each other. As for the others in the Chinese party, they were simply waiting patiently for military reinforcements to arrive from Peking before dropping their masks of courtesy. The vanguard of these troops reached the capital in September, almost three weeks after the return from Yatung. Several thousand soldiers took up positions around the perimeter of the city, and began building barracks for themselves and for those who would follow. Suspicion and mistrust were intense and mutual, though not yet expressed openly. But in the tiny streets of the old quarters of the city, posters with incisive verses began to appear, both expressing and amplifying popular displeasure, which did not bode particularly well for cordial relations between the two peoples.

This fragile truce could not last much longer, and the situation began to deteriorate seriously at the end of October, when about three thousand more Chinese troops arrived in the city. This was becoming all but intolerable to the Tibetans, who now widely repeated the old proverb: "When you see a Chinese coming, there are always at least ten more behind him." Unfortunately, the ancestral proverb turned out to be all too true—in the following months military vehicles continued to arrive and disgorge some twenty thousand more soldiers into the City of the Gods. This created a severe strain on the local ecology and economy, which had always been fragile, subject to seasonal variations and pilgrimage holidays. Huge military camps and barracks did not fit into the equation, and began to upset the balance.

For the first time in its history, Tibet found itself faced with the threat of famine. The authorities had neither the reserves nor the means to satisfy the ever-growing demands of the Chinese military chiefs to provide food for their troops. In the countryside, farmers were protesting. In Lhassa, citizens were complaining about the soaring prices—this was the first time they had ever experienced the phenomenon of inflation. In the monasteries, the formidable guardian corps of monks who maintained order, known as the *dobdob*, suddenly began to receive an unprecedented number of applications from candidates who wanted to learn martial arts.

The situation was further aggravated by Chinese ignorance of Tibetan customs and mores. Besides the unrest created by the deteriorating economy, their disregard and contempt for local customs probably gave equal offense. For Tibetans, Lhassa is a sacred city. Among other things, this means that animals must not be killed within its precincts—yet the Chinese did this without hesitation, including burning their bones. In the streets Tibetans now began to harass the occupiers, and sometimes children threw stones at them. The satirical verses now appeared everywhere, and dealt with every aspect of the situation, from the pomposity of the officers to the falsity of Chinese promises and hypocrisy of their pretensions of "liberation."

General Chang finally demanded that the Tibetan government suppress these tracts, posters, and even songs, claiming that they were part of a "reactionary conspiracy." The Tibetan reaction to this was at first one of incredulity, then laughter, and finally bitter denunciations in the course of many large and spontaneous meetings, where people demanded reparations and the withdrawal of foreign troops. As for the local aristocracy, their conspicuous lack of bravery in facing up to the challenge was the subject of another type of graffiti. A public resolution was formally adopted, with one copy sent to the *kashag*, and another to the Chinese command. This infuriated the Chinese officials, further widening the gap between locals and occupiers.

In violation of their own Seventeen Point Agreement itself, Peking now began to send dozens of high officials and bureaucrats to take charge of Tibetan affairs. The governor multiplied their meetings, and insisted that the members of the Tibetan cabinet attend them all—yet without being able to say a word about their decisions. But one day, when the demands of these officials (whom they regarded as, if not yet enemies, then at least as intruders) became truly exorbitant, Lukhangwa, the chief secular minister, calmly informed the Chinese that these demands were unrealistic, and that they could not expect to have them met.

According to him, the balance between the needs of the indigenous population and the resources of the government was already in danger of collapsing, and their dwindling surplus was not sufficient to feed the Chinese troops for more than one or two more months at the outside. And he boldly added that in any case he saw no necessity for so many troops in the capital. If their purpose was supposedly to defend the country, then they should be sent to the border areas. A small number of officers and their lieutenants would be plenty to accomplish the task in Lhassa.

The Chinese governor at first reacted with relative politeness, yet refused to budge from his position that it was the Tibetan government which had asked China to send its troops, so as to protect the Roof of the World from "foreign imperialist ambitions." Therefore it was the entire responsibility of the Tibetans to guarantee them food and shelter.

The dialogue between the two communities then began to further deteriorate, from polite rebuttals to heated disputes. This worried the Dalai Lama, yet he felt that the time was not yet right for him to intervene, though he did make an effort to rein in the tempers of his officials, so as not to further inflame the situation. Meanwhile, the openly increasing popular resentment only fed the

Chinese officials' arrogance. They finally accused the Tibetan ministers of a "plot to subvert the Seventeen Point Agreement." They were unable or unwilling to understand that the Tibetan people did not want the "help" being offered by Peking, and that they wanted to govern their own country, even though many admitted the need for reforms so as to move more into the reality of the modern world. But some Chinese officials now began to perceive that in order to manage the Tibetans, they would have to deal more directly with the Dalai Lama. They were getting a better sense of his extreme importance for all Tibetans, though they understood nothing of the basis of the intimate relationship between this unique monarch and his people.

Keeping himself informed of the minutest details of the calamity which was preparing to engulf his country, the Dalai Lama became exhausted, and returned to his studies for solace. One of the memorable events of this period was when he was looking through his telescope from the heights of the Potala, and observed the laborious approach of an endless procession of Chinese soldiers.

> They entered the city with a huge unfurling of red flags and a fanfare of trumpets and tubas, displaying posters of Mao and his second in command, Chao Teh. It was very impressive, as if these soldiers had emerged straight from hell. [...] A bit later, I noticed that they were in a pitiful state. They all seemed undernourished, and their uniforms were in rags. In the everlasting dust of the Tibetan plains, it was their emaciated look which gave them such a dreadful aspect.[33]

This was also the occasion of an unforgettable incident which wryly symbolized the vast psychological and cultural gap between the two peoples. As the Chinese soldiers entered into Lhassa with their noisy fanfare, they were pleasantly surprised to be met by a

---

[33] Tenzin Gyatso, *Au loin la liberté* (Paris: Fayard, 1990).

large crowd of Tibetans applauding vigorously. However, the decidedly grim expressions on their faces were in puzzling contrast to the applause. What they didn't know is that in Tibetan custom such clapping of hands is a gesture meant to ward off demons...

It was during this period that Tenzin Gyatso began a profound study of the *Lam Rim,* or "Steps on the Way to Awakening," a fundamental work by Tsong-Khapa, the great reformer and founder of the Gelugpa school to which the Dalai Lamas belonged. Since the age of eight, Tenzin Gyatso had been familiarizing himself little by little with the tantric teachings, along with the more traditional monastic curriculum. The *Lam Rim* offered the keys to extremely precise mental exercises which, along with an intensive practice of meditation, were supposed to be a decisive aid towards Awakening. His two mentors continued to guide him in esoteric teachings which are only transmitted directly from masters to a very limited number of initiates.

After the death of his faithful janitor came that of another major figure of his childhood, Taktra Rinpoche, the ex-regent. At the time the young sovereign happened to be engaged in a very strict annual meditation retreat, and was unable to attend the cremation ceremony. Some weeks later, he personally directed the long consecration ceremony of the memorial *stupa*[34] of this man who had been one of his first masters.

The political situation continued its inexorable deterioration, and the Dalai Lama spared no effort in trying to keep up the morale of his close official associates, who were devastated by the futility of their attempts to reason with the invaders, while the climate of revolt was growing all around them.

In spite of formal governmental injunctions to avoid offending the Chinese, tracts and posters flourished in the city, and they pulled no punches. General Chang threw a tantrum about this, accusing the two chief ministers of being "imperialists guilty of conspiracy."

---

[34] *Stupa* is a Buddhist stone shrine, varying greatly in size and function, yet having the characteristic form of a kind of modified pyramid.

He attempted to get rid of them by demanding that from now on he would deal only with the Dalai Lama alone. But the young man refused. However, this refusal was not sustainable. One day, during one of the increasingly stormy discussions between the governor and the ministers in the presence of the Dalai Lama, the former totally lost his temper because of an acid remark by Lobsang Tashi, and made as if to attack him physically. Appalled by this behavior, the Dalai Lama intervened to prevent disaster. But from then on, he was obliged to receive them separately for the most part.

Some group meetings still took place, and one of these took a bad turn when General Chang announced that the only topic for the day was the impending integration of the Tibetan army into the Chinese army. The chief civil minister replied that this would never be, because no matter what the Seventeen Point Agreement supposedly said, the Chinese themselves had violated it so many times that it now had no more validity. To this the General retorted that all Tibetan flags were to be replaced by the red-starred flag of Communist China. To which the other vehemently replied: "If you do, it will be burned. That will make you look good!" And Lukhangwa added, "Do you really imagine that the best moment to ask someone to be your friend is when you've just bashed him on the head?" The discussion ended there, and the General left, pale with rage.

After this came a Chinese report condemning the behavior of the ministers. Caught in the middle, the Dalai Lama felt his only recourse was to have his two ministers resign, in order to save their lives. This led to a relative truce for several months, and Tenzin Gyatso took advantage of it by working on needed reforms. It was also during this period that the tenth Panchen Lama returned to Tibet under heavy Chinese escort. Chökyi Gyaltsen, the second highest dignitary of Tibetan Buddhism, had been born in 1938 in Xunhua county, in the province of Chinghaï, which was already under Chinese control. He had been officially "recognized" in June, 1944 by the former nationalist regime, whereas the Tibetan ecclesiastical authority had chosen another child from Kham province.

The youth had been brought up in Tashilhumpo at Shigatse, the traditional seat of the lineage.

But the nationalists had succeeded in imposing their protégé, and the communists unhesitatingly adopted this legacy of their enemies, and attempted to condition the youth in their ideology. During the first meeting between this Panchen Lama and the Dalai Lama, who was only three years his senior, it was noticed that some kind of mysterious current seemed to pass between the two adolescents. The Panchen Lama showed a marked deference towards the Dalai Lama. This was not at all to the liking of his protectors, who pressed him to leave as soon as possible after the official audience and a private dinner between him and the Dalai Lama at the Potala.

Precarious though it was, the truce gave the Dalai Lama enough time to give his full attention to the reforms which he had been planning ever since his retreat at Dromo. He was especially concerned with education and the judicial system, which he considered totally unadapted to the times. During his travels he had also noted the need for major improvements of a road system which had practically ceased to exist, so as to facilitate travel in the high country. All his ideas arose out of a long-term vision for his country, and his first act was to abolish all hereditary debts, and to suspend repayments of government loans to the poorest people.

Not only did these decrees displease the nobles and certain monastery officials, they also caused an embarrassed reaction from the Chinese authorities, who had a different calendar in mind. They had already started to collectivize lands in Amdo.

In order to convince reluctant farmers of the benefits of this, they invited a delegation to go upon a guided tour in China. But they returned with little enthusiasm for collectivization.

The summer of 1953 marked an important event in the adolescent's life: his initiation in the tradition of *Kalachakra,* the Wheel of Time, one of the highest rituals of tantric Buddhism. This was transmitted to him by his teacher Ling Rinpoche. No one could have suspected at the time that the fourteenth Dalai Lama would one day open up this secret ritual to the entire world, performing Kalachakra initiations in many countries, not only for his own people in exile, but for many thousands of Westerners as well. Tibetan tradition says that this ritual is especially linked to world peace.

At Lhassa in 1953, however, it was a far more complex and arcane version, involving over seven hundred divinities. This teaching demands an arduous and minute preparation of at least a week before each transmission. The public part of the ceremony lasts as long, and is divided into several parts. Although the first steps are open to many people, a formal training is required for the third degree, and is reserved for a small number of adepts, who have also been trained with the aim of someday being able to transmit it themselves.

The Dalai Lama's final, grand Kalachakra initiation did not take place until 1954 in Lhassa. This was just after he had ordered a full ceremony of the *Monlam,* or Great Annual Prayer, to be held at Jokhang, marking the beginning of the Tibetan calendar.

This was the moment the Chinese authorities chose to summon the young sovereign to undertake a long voyage to China. Opinion was very divided among his advisors, for some suspected a trap. But Tenzin Gyatso himself proved to be both willful and curious, and was determined to see with his own eyes what was taking place in China. His secret hope was that his personal rapport with Mao and the other top Chinese leaders would at least convince them to respect their own signed agreements. He had read attentively the reports from members of the mission which had gone there the previous year. Even while he was busy with the Tibetan assembly in working out a new constitution, he held to his plan to go to China. He felt that by accepting it, he had a better chance of gaining at least some autonomy for his people. In an effort to calm his people's fears, he solemnly promised during a huge public ceremony that he would return the following year.

An impressive caravan of about five hundred people finally took to the road. They had nineteen hundred miles to go before reaching Peking. The party included the Dalai Lama's family, his tutors and closest servants, along with monks, counselors, merchants, nobles, and commoners. The date of departure fell in the middle of summer. Although the weather was excellent, spirits were clouded with a heavy anxiety: the Tibetan people feared for the Dalai Lama's life, and did not hide it.

After crossing the Kyi-chu river by means of yak-hide boats, the caravan made its first halt at the famous university-monastery of Ganden, one of the "three pillars" of Tibet. It was perched on the crest of a mountain, at an altitude of over sixteen thousand feet. From the monastery one can behold a magnificent panorama of valleys below. All around its precincts, consisting of sanctuaries, prayer houses, and shrines, the land is bathed in a beautifully clear light. One feels a serene symbiosis between humanity and nature, which moved Giuseppe Tucci to exclaim that to see Ganden was to see "a vision of something beyond this world."

Enthused by his first visit to this place, the Dalai Lama spent several days there, visiting sites, holding audiences, giving brief teachings, and participating in the monastic routine in an atmosphere which was solemn and mindful. He clearly remembers a strange occurrence there which he is unable to explain to this day. In the pantheon of Tibetan divinities, there is one with the head of a buffalo, regarded as one of the most fearsome protectors of the dharma. Shortly after his arrival at Ganden, he entered the shrine room where there was a statue of this divinity, in order to present his respects. He noticed that the head of the statue was bent towards the ground, as if to symbolize allegiance or deference. Shortly before taking his leave of Ganden, the Dalai Lama returned to this shrine, following the custom of placing a *khata* scarf before the statue. He was astonished to see that this time the head of the statue was no longer bent towards the ground, but was turned towards the east, displaying an expression of unmistakable ferocity.

The following days were not easy ones. Storms had demolished the Chinese-made roads across the Kongpo, and snowmelt and rains had brought mudslides, so that even the mules stumbled and slid

First meeting with Mao Tse-tung in Peking.

on the precarious ground. The leaders of the Chinese escort which had joined them were stubborn in their efforts to continue along this road which no longer existed, whereas the Tibetan guides sought in vain to convince them that it would be better to take the traditional high roads. This obstinacy cost the lives of three Chinese soldiers and several mules, carried away by an avalanche.

Whereas the Dalai Lama wanted to make stops in monasteries or hermitages, the Chinese itinerary was one of successive halts in military camps, where soldiers on watch never failed to come out waving tiny red flags made of paper. After three weeks of marching under these conditions, the rather ragged and travel-weary caravan finally reached the Poyul, where the road became fully usable. Jeeps and trucks were waiting to transport the entire party to Chengdu, passing through a Chamdo province which was now entirely occupied by the Chinese.

After leaving the town of Dar-tse-do (Tat-sien-lu), the traditional border crossing between Tibet and China, the Dalai Lama was struck by the difference in terrain: they were already descending fast from the Tibetan heights to the low Chinese plains. He remembers wondering about whether the striking differences between the two peoples might be connected with the strong contrast in their geographies. At Chengdu, a bad fever confined him to his bed for several days. Barely recovered, his convoy left again for Shingang, where the Panchen Lama and his entourage joined them.

An old airplane transported the main dignitaries to Xian. This first experience of air travel excited the curiosity of the adolescent, though today he admits to being slightly mistrustful of this means of travel. The remainder of the trip from the ancient imperial capital to Peking was by rail, with special luxury cars which included bathrooms and dining rooms. As they approached the capital, the youth felt occasional twinges of apprehension.

The first welcome was courteous and lavish, obviously designed to impress. The Dalai Lama was carefully observing everything, and although the quantity and quality of the banquet which was served on the evening of their arrival were spectacular, the welcome speech by Chou Teh worried him. The Marshall emphasized Tibet's reunion with the "mother country," and the promise that the Chinese government would do its best to help it to develop and progress. Similar remarks were made by Mao himself two days later, during the course of a meeting which included Liu Shao-shi.

The young Dalai Lama was genuinely impressed by the personality of Mao Tse-tung, with whom he had several meetings. No doubt the latter's well-known charisma was in full force.

> His entire personality exuded authority. His mere presence imposed a kind of respect. And I sensed that he was quite sincere in his seeming determination.[35]

Yet this did not prevent the Dalai Lama from being disturbed by the contradictions which he perceived in the speech of the communist leader. He has never forgotten the latter's specific promises which were broken—for example, that the Chinese generals posted in Lhassa were not to impose their own law, and were only there to guarantee that the previous agreements were respected.

Mao even went so far as to affirm that "Nothing will be undertaken without the Tibetans' consent." This encouraged the Dalai Lama to hope that good relations might be possible after all between Tibet and its giant neighbor. But he was very uneasy about the implications of the communists' radically materialist view of human nature. He also had the impression that even though Mao himself was sincere, his most powerful colleagues were mostly not.

For example, Chou En-lai left the youth with a mixed impression:

> He was all smiles, charm, and wit. But his politeness was so extreme that one wondered if he were to be trusted—in other words, too polite to be honest. During our first meeting, I

---

[35] Tenzin Gyatso, *Au loin la liberté* (Paris: Fayard, 1990).

perceived his great intelligence and insight. But I also had the feeling that he was a person who was inflexible and head-strong in his leadership.[36]

During these six weeks in Peking, filled with lavish banquets and long, boring meetings, the Dalai Lama had occasion to meet some famous political personalities of the day. Nikita Khrushchev and Nikolai Bulganin struck him as drab figures, but his most painful disappointment was his meeting with Jawaharlal Nehru, during an official reception. He had laid great hope in this highly respected man—too much hope.

At a distance Jawaharlal Nehru seemed quite gracious, eas-ily finding friendly words to say to everyone. But when my turn came to shake his hand, he seemed to freeze. He lost his voice, and his eyes seemed to go blank. I felt quite ill at ease, and to break the ice, I told him that I was very happy to meet him, and that in spite of the remoteness of my country, I had heard much about him. He then finally decided to open his mouth, but it was only to say something utterly banal.[37]

When winter came, the Dalai Lama and his entourage began a carefully prepared and guided tour of China. Their hosts were determined to show off their achievements in industrial develop-ment and the happiness of the people due to the boon of com-munism. His mind and senses ever alert, the young sovereign showed a keen interest in everything he saw, from hydroelectric plants to an old rusted battleship in Manchuria.

But Tenzin Gyatso was not long in perceiving the other side of this picture:

---

[36] Tenzin Gyatso, *Mon pays et mon peuple* (Geneva: Olizane, 1984).

[37] Tenzin Gyatso, *Au loin la liberté* (Paris: Fayard, 1990).

There was a grey and humorless fog of conformity everywhere. Occasionally, a flourish of the traditional charm and
courtesy of old China would break through, like an unexpected and welcome ray of sunshine.[38]

Returning to Peking he was just in time to celebrate Losar, the
Tibetan new year. A banquet was held which was attended by Mao,
Chou En-lai, and Chou Teh. Finally the month of March had arrived,
and it was time to return to Lhassa, to the great relief of the Tibetans
in this strange voyage. On the eve of their departure, the Dalai Lama
attended a final meeting with the director of the Central Committee of the Chinese Communist Party, who was supposed to be laying
the foundations for a preparatory Commission for the Autonomous
Region of Tibet. This offered him a ray of hope which he kept in
his heart, but perhaps without being able to really believe it.

Crossing the Tibetan border, the many halts on the road of
return offered abundant evidence of the harsh reality of the occupation. Unhappiness was growing among his people, and there was
great disruption in their lives. His fundamental optimism received
a sharp blow, and he now found himself working hard just to try
to preserve the little that could be preserved. Rumors of armed
resistance reached him, but he foresaw the futility of it. He admired
the ferocious courage and determination of these Tibetan warriors,
but he was all too aware now of the cruel disparity of forces between
them and the Chinese. This only reinforced his original conviction
to avoid bloodshed. He knew that armed combat was hopeless in
the long run.

An unshakable faith that goes to the depths of one's soul is surely
required for anyone who perseveres through the many obstacles on
this path of peace. Each step he took during this spring of 1955 gave
evidence which could only feed doubt and discouragement. Lies
and base manipulations on the part of the Chinese now prevented

---

[38] Tenzin Gyatso, *Mon pays et mon peuple* (Geneva: Olizane, 1984).

him from meeting freely with the Tibetan people. He began to understand that the paranoia for his safety which Chinese officials were now manifesting was nothing but a reflection of their own incomprehension and incompetence in dealing with the Tibetan mentality. They finally arrived at Lhassa in June, which brought a mixture of relief and new worries.

In the Tibetan capital, the previous tensions had abated, giving way to a mood of resignation. Yet ever more alarming news was coming from Kham and Amdo provinces, where the Chinese authorities were imposing their reforms with great brutality. Taxes were soaring, monastery property being especially heavily hit, and nomadic tribes were having to abandon their ancient traditions of following the seasons with their herds, and being settled by force. All this coercion was systematically accompanied by efforts to indoctrinate the population in communist ideology, but this only irritated them further. In early autumn the Chinese authorities decided to try to disarm the Khampa warriors, but these fierce tribes took to the hills. Meanwhile the mounting misery in the countryside was causing entire villages to empty, and Lhassa began to swell with peasant and nomad refugees.

Accounts of torture, brutality, and vile mistreatment were growing like wildfire. Disgust was also evoked by the Chinese convocations of public "self-criticism" meetings for the "re-education" of the people. The Dalai Lama could scarcely believe the horrors that now reached his ears—hanging by the feet, dismemberment, decapitations—he simply could not understand the process by which human beings become transformed into something far worse than savage beasts in their treatment of each other.

Reports of these atrocities committed by the occupiers could only rile the Tibetan people, and they now began to seriously protest. Preparations for the new year and the Monlam festival were a pretext for unusual meetings between different groups of people, and these led to many apparently fortuitous encounters. Some prominent citizens began to collect funds for organizing a spontaneous popular ceremony of offerings to protective divinities, so as to assure a long and prosperous life for the Dalai Lama. But this also turned out to be a clever cover for the preparation and foundation of a resistance movement, the Chushi Gangdruk ("Four Rivers, Six Mountain Ranges"), which was the Tibetan name for the occupied provinces of Kham and Amdo.

The supposed preparatory Commission for the Autonomous Region of Tibet soon proved to be another source of dismay. Headed by Peking robots who merely followed central government orders, this institution of "democratic centralism" afforded an instructive example of the bogus, manipulated majority. The Dalai Lama saw this, but hoped that the presence of Tibetans on this Commission would influence the balance for the better. But his hopes faded fast. As soon as the first measures began to be declared, the Tibetans rose up in alarm and denounced them as a radical attack on the very foundations of their lives. They refused to even consider adopting them. In the streets of Lhassa, anger mounted once more, with petitions circulating everywhere. This time leaders emerged who did not mince words: they openly demanded the immediate withdrawal of the Chinese, and proclaimed the slogan "Tibet for the Tibetans."

Tracts and spontaneous gatherings multiplied, to the great consternation of the Chinese. Even the Great Prayer festivals were tinged with politics, something unprecedented in Lhassan memory. Nevertheless, the young Dalai Lama led the rituals with confidence and grace. But this holiday season was darkened by rumors from the provinces: frequent armed skirmishes, increasing pressure on local leaders to institute totally unacceptable reforms, and outright battles between Tibetans and Chinese.

Considered as hotbeds of resistance, monasteries were now under heavy Chinese surveillance, especially in the eastern areas, where the invaders seemed to consider the country completely conquered.

As the atmosphere became still heavier, the Dalai Lama thought often of the grim prophecy of his predecessor, and told himself that the time of darkness was indeed at hand.

Curiously, during his traditional trance on the occasion of the new year, the Nechung oracle had concluded his divination by the following cryptic words: "The light of the Wish-Fulfilling Jewel will shine one day upon the West."

Pilgrimage to India

The Chinese noose on Tibet now tightened with the construction of a small airport and new roads which permitted troops to arrive in much greater numbers. Every day the Dalai Lama contemplated the situation, and saw that in spite of all his goodwill, he could do nothing about it. His later assessment was candid:

> This preparatory Commission was nothing but a travesty of responsible government. I saw little hope of success in the future now. Even worse, I had the feeling of losing the leadership of my own people.[39]

The Chinese were also busy building a hotel in Lhassa for their official guests, a building with public baths, and a huge meeting hall, right at the foot of the Potala. Typical Chinese arched roofs now began to rise up in the Tibetan capital.

In April of 1956, Marshall Chen Yi himself came to visit, leading an impressive delegation whose task was to set up new administrative structures. From this point on it became very clear that there were flagrant contradictions between the promises of the Seventeen Point Agreement and the reality of its implementation. The so-called autonomy was a fraud. Tibetan institutions were being reduced to impotent facades, and all real decisions were being made by Chinese authorities, with the occasional collaboration of some Tibetan

---

[39] Tenzin Gyatso, *Mon pays et mon peuple* (Geneva: Olizane, 1984).

"representatives," who were in reality puppets to be brought out publicly only when absolutely necessary—for example, to deceive foreign visitors. These pseudo-consultations of Tibetan officials regarding their own affairs finally provoked the latter to emit scathing denials and to engage in passive resistance. The Chinese had not foreseen this obstacle, and they responded with the only tactic they knew: repression.

In spite of these oppressive conditions, the Dalai Lama continued his practice and training with a seeming imperturbability. At the same time, his character was being formed by his arduous dealings with Chinese officials, with whom he strove to his utmost to obtain at least some breathing space for his people. But his labor was mostly in vain: they already had their orders from Peking, and they carried them out emotionlessly, with no apparent concern for the pain they inflicted. Yet Tenzin Gyatso was still reluctant to credit many of the reports of extreme cruelty that were now coming in— until the day that a copy of a newspaper from Kham, published at Karze by the Chinese authorities for the edification of the people, reached his hands. There he saw a photograph of severed heads of "reactionary criminals," according to the caption. Now he could no longer doubt the horror of the situation. He still remembers the appalled reaction of his brother Lobsang Samten, recounting how the Chinese head of security had one day politely inquired of him as to how to say "Kill him!" in Tibetan.

For his own peace of mind, he used a pretext of traditional rituals and festival ceremonies so as to leave Lhassa as often as possible. Thus he was able to have several days at a time free of obligatory consultations with Chinese officials, which was coming to be both a futile and an extremely disagreeable exercise. He was also waiting expectantly to finally be able to go to India, accepting the invitation of the Maharaja of Sikkim, who had visited him just after the Tibetan new year. The invitation was officially on behalf of the Mahabodhi Society, which was organizing celebrations of the twenty-five hundredth anniversary of the birth of Gautama Shakyamuni Buddha.

For Tenzin Gyatso this was the realization of a dream: to perform a full pilgrimage in the holy land of the Buddha, and meditate in the very places where he walked in his human incarnation. He also still hoped for a better meeting with Nehru and other Indian leaders, for he could not rid himself of the belief that these men must surely be in some sense the heirs of Mahatma Gandhi. But of this he spoke to no one.

However, the Chinese had another view of this plan. General Fan Ming, who was replacing General Chang while he was in China, was hostile to it. Given the current workload of the preparatory Commission, how could he think of taking off at this time? Also, India was a doubtful country, with many reactionaries, and if something were to happen to the Dalai Lama there, who would be responsible? Furthermore, an invitation from a religious organization did not constitute an official request (forgetting, of course, that for the Dalai Lama religious duty is foremost).

During this time the situation was becoming still worse in the eastern territories where the Chinese occupation was the most complete. Sporadic revolts broke out in Kham and Amdo, and frequent battles were making blood and violence a part of daily life. The Dalai Lama began to reconsider his plan of going to India, and appointed Trijang Rinpoche to accept the invitation in his place.

However, General Chang returned to Lhassa that autumn, and announced that the Chinese government was no longer opposed to his pilgrimage. However, he lectured the Dalai Lama about caution. Since UNESCO was a sponsor of the event,[40] he urged the Dalai Lama to beware of likely approaches by individuals or groups intent on fomenting trouble for China. He especially insisted that in the event of any participation in the festivities by representatives of the regime in Taiwan, the Dalai Lama immediately leave the premises. In any case, the Chinese ambassador in New Delhi would be there

---

[40] Communist China was at that time excluded from membership in the United Nations.

to keep an eye on things. And he finished his lecture with a threat: "If you ever feel tempted to have any dealings with those people, just remember what happened to Hungary and Poland." The warning was clear, even for a young monk-sovereign of a remote country where he himself felt a prisoner.

Later Tenzin Gyatso learned that Jawaharlal Nehru himself had officially intervened with the Chinese on the subject of the Dalai Lama's pilgrimage. The news of the previous refusal had spread rapidly, thanks to the concerted efforts of the Indian consul in Tibet. The immediate reaction in major Buddhist centers all over the world was one of indignation that the Dalai Lama would be forbidden to make such an important pilgrimage for a Buddhist. Rather than see this indignation turn to widespread Asian anger at Peking, and risk an upset of the already fragile balance between China and India, the Chinese had reversed themselves. But so as not to entirely lose face, they ordered that the Panchen Lama be included in the Tibetan delegation. This group would also include the Dalai Lama's two mentors, his closest servants, and his brothers Lobsang Samten and Tenzin Chögyal.

Duly instructed as to the perils of a reactionary country like India, and told not to express himself freely, but to confine himself to speeches which had been properly censored and approved for him by the Chinese, the Dalai Lama left Lhassa in November, 1956. With his small entourage, he traveled by automobile on the traditional route which led to Sikkim via the Chumbi river valley. The Panchen Lama joined the group at Shigatse, and the Chinese escort left them at the last town before the Nathu pass, seeming visibly worried about allowing this small party to go into the great unknown without them. General Tin Ming-yi, commander of the escort, repeated the instructions to the Dalai Lama, placing special emphasis on the great benefits which Tibet had experienced since its "peaceful liberation" by their Chinese brothers.

After switching from automobile to horses, the travelers breathed a sigh of relief, and began to feel like real pilgrims at last: they were following the ancestral road which traversed the Himalayan range towards the Buddhist holy land. Halting at the pass, they gathered before the great cairn surrounded by prayer flags, and each added their stone to the cairn. Like his companions, the Dalai Lama filled his lungs and gave a great shout into the immensity, pronouncing the traditional homage: *Lha Gyal-lo!* ("Victory to the Gods!") He still remembers the luxurious natural beauty of this place, with its rhododendron and pine forests, with yellow poppies, larkspurs, and monkshood flowers. This was the most verdant part of the Chumbi valley, a natural park which botanists and hikers regard as a paradise.

During their descent of the southern slopes of the Himalayas, the party was met and given a warm welcome by a committee which included the Maharaja of Sikkim himself, accompanied by the former Indian consul at Lhassa, and Kazi Sonam Topgyal, who was to serve as faithful interpreter for the entire voyage. A halt had been arranged in a tiny village near Lake Tsongpo, and after a morning of climbing towards the lake in bright sunshine, snow suddenly began to fall. For Tibetans, this is a good omen.

That evening in the village, the Dalai Lama was pleasantly surprised to find his two older brothers, Taktser Rinpoche and Gyalo Thondup. They had left Tibet during an earlier stage of the Chinese invasion, and each had been working in his own way to seek outside support to prevent their country from being consumed by the dragon. For the first time, all five brothers found themselves all together, and they were joined some days later by their mother and two sisters. The entire family was thus able to come together to celebrate this great Buddhist pilgrimage.

The next day the small group rode on ponies to Gangtok, at that time capital of the independent nation of Sikkim. An enormous crowd had gathered to greet the young emanation of Avalokiteshvara, revered throughout the Himalayas. But just before reaching the city they were met by the Jeeps of the Chinese ambassador and his retinue, who insisted they ride in their automobiles, symbols of modern progress.

They stayed only one more night in Sikkim, enough time for a banquet and a brief rest, before continuing their descent into the warm plains of India, and the Bagdogra airport, where a special plane had been chartered to fly this distinguished party to Delhi.

The Dalai Lama took advantage of the varied phases of this trip to reflect, with his characteristic habit of drawing comparisons. Although he admitted that modern roads and motorized vehicles shortened voyages impressively, he noted that travel on horseback is far more conducive to reflection and meditation, to say nothing of appreciation of the natural beauty of the country. He noticed that the Indian airplane was more comfortable than the Chinese one in which he had made his first flight, but this seemed but a symbol of the far more important difference in welcome, which was warm and genuine on the part of the Indians.

His Chinese voyage the previous year had been his first experience of life in a foreign country, and one full of luxury in that case, but he felt immediately more relaxed and at home in India. He felt at ease in the atmosphere of sincere friendliness he found there, whereas the scrupulous formalities of respect of the Chinese had generated a stiff and unnatural atmosphere during the most minor interviews. Already, the quality and tone of a conversation, beyond its verbal content, had become of fundamental importance to the Dalai Lama.

He retains many anecdotes of this voyage. For example, they crossed the Gangtok in a car belonging to the Maharaja, ornamented with two small flags, those of Sikkim and of Tibet. Taking advantage of a traffic jam, an unknown Chinese (whom they later discovered was the official interpreter of the embassy there) ran up to the car, tore away the Tibetan flag, and substituted a Chinese red flag. Later, right after the arrival of the airplane in Delhi, the Chinese ambassador appeared and demanded to make an unscheduled opening speech to the diplomats present, among whom were Nehru and the vice-president, Radhakrishna. After some moments of awkward consultation, it was made known that representatives

New Delhi, 1956: A family reunion with the Dalai Lama and his mother, brothers, and sisters. From left to right: his mother, Gyaymo Chenmo (1900–1981); Tsering Dolma (1919–1964); Thubten Jigme Norbu [Taktser Rinpoche] (b. 1922); Gyalo Thondup (b. 1928); Lobsang Samten (1933–1985); Tenzin Gyatso [fourteenth Dalai Lama] (b. 1935); Jetsun Pena (b. 1941); Tenzin Chögyal [Ngari Rinpoche] (b. 1946).

of Great Britain and the United States had also been invited, and were present. As if by magic, the Chinese ambassador vanished. An Indian high official took over and made the speech, a vague smile playing upon his lips.

The Dalai Lama had only recently attained the age of twenty-one, but he was very aware that he must play a game of utmost discretion. Not without a touch of youthful candor, he sought the advice of older and more experienced politicians who had been engaged for years in their own struggles for independence. Right after his arrival in Delhi on November 25, 1956, he was led directly to the president's official residence for a meeting with Rajendra Prasad.

> I discovered an aged man of slow gestures, soft voice, and a perfect humility. Along with his vice-president Radhakrishna, he symbolized for me the ancient spirit of India.[41]

The next morning, his first activity of the day was a visit to Rajghat, where Mahatma Gandhi had been cremated.

> I wondered what precious advice I might have received if he were still alive. I felt deeply that he would have devoted his wholehearted energy and personal charisma in a non-violent campaign for the freedom of the Tibetan people. With deepening fervor, I regretted not being able to meet him in this world. [...] I renewed my decision to follow his example, no matter what the obstacles. And more than ever, I resolved to never associate myself with acts of violence.[42]

For several days the Dalai Lama's time was filled with religious ceremonies, meetings, official banquets, and exchanges of ideas with scholars of different backgrounds. He found solace and support in his conviction that only mutual respect and truthfulness can avail

---

[41] Tenzin Gyatso, *Mon pays et mon peuple* (Geneva: Olizane, 1984).
[42] Ibid.

in the search for solutions to the thorniest problems, and that repression and violence only make conflicts worse. It was during this time that he began to suspect, going against his own fervent hopes, that it might be more reasonable if he were to remain in India, at least as long as there was no sign of positive change in the Chinese policy in Tibet.

> It seemed to me that as long as I was at home, I could no longer render service to my own people—I could not even restrain their desire to have recourse to violence. All my efforts towards a peaceful solution had so far come to nothing. As long as I stayed in India, I could at least bear witness to the entire world as to what was really happening in Tibet, and mobilize moral support for us.[43]

At his first meeting with Nehru, he opened his heart. He gave a frank account of what he knew to be happening in Tibet, and added his impression that the Chinese authorities were bent on permanent destruction of his country, annihilating his people's customs and religion. He hinted that he might like to remain for some time in India. The illustrious Indian prime minister listened to him politely, agreeing with him that it was useless to fight the Chinese militarily. But he advised him strongly to return to his country so as to find a peaceful implementation of the Seventeen Point Agreement. In response, the Dalai Lama exclaimed that his many strenuous efforts towards this very aim had totally failed. Nehru promised to have a word with Chou En-lai, who was expected to arrive in New Delhi the very next day, and try to arrange an interview between him and the Dalai Lama.

He kept his word, and Tenzin Gyatso found himself once more in the company of the same smiling and courteous man, full of charm and duplicity. This time the Dalai Lama told him forthrightly

---

[43] Tenzin Gyatso, *Mon pays et mon peuple* (Geneva: Olizane, 1984).

about his distress at the way the Chinese were governing, not only in Lhassa, but especially in Kham and Amdo, where their attitude was only aggravating popular resentment and revolt. Chou En-lai responded suavely that certainly there must have been mistakes made by the Chinese officials in question, and that he would speak to Mao himself about this. However, he refused make the slightest promise about the situation itself.

A few days later, the Chinese minister convened a private dinner with the two older brothers of the Dalai Lama. This time the exchanges were even more frank, and clearly displeased Chou En-lai. Nevertheless, he reiterated his assurance as to the goodwill of his government, even going so far as to tell them that they were at liberty to remain in India as long as they wished, and to continue to speak in their own frank and critical way about the situation in their country. But at the end of the dinner, Chou En-lai casually remarked that he had heard the Dalai Lama was also thinking of extending his stay in India. And he warned the brothers to urge him to return to Tibet—if he did not, the Tibetan people would risk grave consequences.

Leaving this atmosphere behind, the Dalai Lama now began the pilgrimage of which he had dreamed since early childhood. Sanchi, Ajanta, Benares, Sarnath, and Bodh Gaya are some of the major steps on the path of Buddhism's Indian beginnings. He marveled at the artistic and architectural masterpieces he encountered, and also felt sadness at the signs of violent religious conflict which had damaged some of them. And above all, he recollected himself in devotion, prayer, and meditation in the very places which had marked the life of one individual whose path led to the universal.

At Bodh Gaya, he intensely felt the profound communion among the pilgrims who ceaselessly gathered at the foot of the *bodhi* tree, believed to be planted at the very place where their master had sat when he attained his first great Awakening. From the depths of his heart, he felt a sense of being on familiar ground and of returning to his "spiritual homeland." Previously, their party had stopped in Behar to visit the site of the great Buddhist university of Nalanda, where scholars and sages of ancient times had brought the study and knowledge of the dharma to an unsurpassed level. Now it was all silent ruins. In the eyes of the young monk-pilgrim, this was an opportunity to remember the fundamental Buddhist teaching of the impermanence of all things in time.

At every major stage of their itinerary he was met by thousands of Tibetan exiles. He used the occasion to read sutras (Buddhist sacred verses) especially for them, and to cheer and urge them not to be discouraged by the obstacles facing them.

After a brief stay at Bodh Gaya, Tenzin Gyatso traveled on to Sarnath, near Varanasi (Benares), where the historical Buddha had "set the wheel of the dharma in motion"—meaning that this place, known as the Deer Park, was where he had first given his teaching of the Four Noble Truths. On that day a solemn, calm, and yet joyous procession circumambulated the sanctuary, and the emotion was so intense that tears ran down his cheeks.

> Why did I cry? Because I am a disciple of the Buddha, and these few enshrined relics are all that is left of him. Because this is a reminder of individual responsibility, of the necessity to practice diligently and unceasingly, to follow the teachings and persevere on the Way. Because the human eternity has only a time.[44]

This beautiful serenity itself could not last, of course. An urgent message arrived from General Chang in Lhassa, addressed to the Chinese embassy in Delhi. The situation in Tibet was growing very tense, revolt was underway, fomented by "high-level spies and conspirators." It was urgent for the Dalai Lama to return. One of the Chinese messengers insisted that he come to Delhi soon, so as to meet with Chou En-lai, who was returning there. "In a few days, I

---

[44] Claude B. Levenson, *Le Seigneur du Lotus blanc* (Paris: Livre de Poche, 1989).

would have to plunge back into the world of politics, hatred, and mistrust," he later wrote.[45]

He had no choice but to go to this meeting. Yet Chou En-lai proved to be as evasive as ever. The Chinese leader confirmed the reports of a worsening of the situation at Lhassa, and made no secret of Peking's intentions to use repressive measures. The Dalai Lama repeated his criticisms and comments on the suffering of his people, adding that there might still be a chance for understanding, provided that the imposed hardships and tortures stop. Chou En-lai replied that Mao himself had just made a public guarantee that "Democratic reforms will not be imposed in Tibet against the will of the people."

Having caught wind of the invitation the Dalai Lama had received to visit Bhutan before returning to Lhassa, he emphasized that in his opinion this detour was unjustified, and he formally advised him not to accept it. And he added a veiled warning against "Indian officials who behave strangely," and also against "troublemakers," though he refrained from specifying their identity or intentions. The Dalai Lama said that he would reflect upon this conversation, but for the moment he had nothing more to say.

In the loneliness of his youth and conscience, Tenzin Gyatso pondered the contradictory ideas which assailed him. He strove to consider objectively all the diverse points of view, including the implications of his own attitude, so as to judge the overall situation. He opened himself one last time to Nehru, who urged him to return and to have confidence in Chou En-lai's promises, practically guaranteeing the good faith of the latter.

As if to buttress his assurances further, Mao gave a public speech on February 7, 1957, in which he declared that Tibet was not yet ready for the reforms, and that the new agricultural law would be postponed for six years. If at the end of that time the Tibetans still did not want it, the changes would be further postponed, for as long

---

[45] Tenzin Gyatso, *Mon pays et mon peuple* (Geneva: Olizane, 1984).

as fifteen or even fifty years. At the same time the Chinese authorities in Lhassa announced that the work of the preparatory Commission of the Autonomous Region of Tibet was to be put on hold, with a marked reduction of its personnel. These words greatly placated international opinion. But it seemed too good to be true, and the Dalai Lama himself was not fully convinced.

As for his trip to Kalimpong in Bhutan, Nehru at first seemed to agree with Chou En-lai, but then suddenly reversed himself, declaring that India is a free country, and if the Dalai Lama saw fit to visit Kalimpong, he was welcome to do so. He added that the Indian government would do everything to assure that the trip take place under the best conditions. The Dalai Lama thanked him, and invited the Indian prime minister to visit Lhassa. Nehru promised to do so early in the following year.

In mid-February, 1957, Tenzin Gyatso and his family set off for Calcutta, traveling by train. A few days later, a plane flew them to Bagdogra, and the last leg of the trip to Kalimpong was by Jeep, along a winding and narrow road. They were lodged at the House of Bhutan, as guests of Rani Chuni Dorje, mother of the former prime minister of the Country of the Thunder-Dragon. Curiously, the thirteenth Dalai Lama had also found refuge here during his own brief exile in India.

A lively commercial center, Kalimpong was one of the most colorful stops along the eastern trans-Himalayan route. Wealthy landowners kept houses there so as to escape the sweltering heat of the monsoon season in the plains just below, and merchants and mule-drivers rubbed shoulders in the constant cheerful chaos of its streets. It was also known as a useful reconnaissance center for adventurers, spies, and lovers of the most shady kinds of intrigue.

The Dalai Lama spent a week there, dividing his time between reflection and public teaching, somewhat torn between his religious duties and his worries about a political responsibility which he did not feel he had mastered. Arguments around him grew heated as to the advisability of his return to Lhassa. But he had already made his choice to follow the advice of Nehru and give one more chance to the Chinese to make good on their new promises. As relayed to him by Chou En-lai, Mao's new assurances seemed to be a guarantee of mutual respect and understanding.

Some of those closest to him were of an entirely different opinion, especially his two older brothers. Taktser Rinpoche, who could never forget his firsthand experience of the actions of the invaders in Amdo, felt that the word of the Chinese communists could never be trusted. Even more adamant, Gyalo Thondup believed that every means, including armed struggle, should be used in order to oppose the invasion. Both of them were counting on external help, perhaps from Britain, but especially from the U.S., for the strong declarations of the latter in favor of democracy and respect for human rights had deeply impressed them.

Under discreet cover of his pilgrimage, the secular ex-prime minister Lukhangwa, who had been expelled by the Chinese, arrived quietly in Kalimpong. He was in a hurry to inform the Dalai Lama of what was happening in Lhassa. Without reserve, he expressed his agreement with the point of view of the two older brothers. All three now tried to convince the young sovereign to remain in India, at least temporarily. They even went so far as to pressure him through the Tibetan council of ministers, attempting to obtain a decree from them ordering him to remain in India.

But their efforts were in vain. He was convinced that his place was with his people, and that to remain in India now would not be worthy of his divine representation as Protector of Tibet. News also reached him of consultations of two of the three main oracles, those of Nechung and Gadong, and these confirmed his decision: he must return. His older brothers did not follow him.

As if nature herself wanted to give him more time for reflection, a heavy blizzard began to fall when his party arrived at Gangtok, closing all the passes. For an entire month the roads remained blocked. Peking now became anxious about this state of affairs, and dispatched both the Panchen Lama and their puppet Ngabo

Ngawang Jigme to Tibet. The latter was the former governor of Chamdo who had changed sides during the invasion and signed the infamous Seventeen Point Agreement.

The Dalai Lama remained as the guest of the Maharaja of Sikkim and filled this time of waiting with meditation and public teaching. Later, he recalled of this period:

> I was weary of all the political activity. All these meetings had filled my time at Delhi, and forced me to shorten my pilgrimage. I had come to the point of loathing all these words, and would even have retired permanently from public affairs, had it not been for my duty to the Tibetan people.

After the caravan finally set off, they soon reached the pass of Nathu-La. Just before crossing over the high point which marks the Tibetan border, the party felt a strange heaviness in the air, despite the clear sky. Everyone was wondering what the future held, though no one spoke about it.

Revolt and Exile

Down the road from the Nathu-La pass to Lhassa, the caravan made time for several stops: Dromo/Yatung (where the adolescent Dalai Lama had taken refuge during the early part of the Chinese invasion), Gyantse, and Shigatse. During all this time, he endeavored to calm apprehensions, but the news which was reaching them was far from good. And even he still had doubts as to whether his decision would turn out to be the wisest one. But he hoped against hope that he would be able to help. He did not give major consideration to the duplicity of politicians, nor to the motives and interests which drove the international arena into which he wished to integrate his country.

With noble steadfastness in spite of his own and others' doubts, the young head of state constantly repeated what he had been saying since his return from China, now reinforced by the recent promises he had received in India: "The Chinese are not our rulers, and we are not their subjects." He endeavored to hold strictly to the letter of the Seventeen Point Agreement, as Nehru had counseled him to do, and often didactically reiterated this policy to others. He even complied when the Chinese demanded of him that he send an envoy to Amdo in order to convince the rebels to lay down their arms, hoping to stop the cycle of bloodshed.

But enmities were now running deep, and some of the occupiers' tactics surpassed the worst tortures described in Buddhist or other hell-realms. However, in spite of all these atrocities, the Dalai Lama still held to his belief in the possibility of an autonomy for his country which would at least preserve the special character of its people and civilization, if not their independence. During this time the Chinese officials in Lhassa were obeying the recent instructions from Peking, and for a period following Mao's speech about the postponement of the reforms, there was a respite. But hardly had the truce begun when the situation worsened once again, as open revolt broke out in the eastern provinces.

Upon his return to Lhassa, he found the city apparently the same, except for the increasing number of refugees from battle zones, seeking a governmental protection which would soon prove to be a cruel illusion. In those zones, a handful of daring and heroic Tibetan chieftains were leading men and women in battle, sometimes inflicting heavy losses on the Chinese. But external aid was minimal, and old local rivalries also undermined the Tibetan cause. The Chinese skillfully exploited these differences, but military leaders were forced to admit that the rebellion posed a very serious problem for them. They demanded that Tibetan leaders intervene to end it, yet offered no concessions in return, continuing to violate the terms of the Seventeen Point Agreement.

Given the vast difference in military force, Tibetan options were few indeed. Theoretically, authority resided in the *kashag* (council of ministers) and in the Dalai Lama, but in reality their hands were tied by the Chinese military presence, with major decisions now being made in Peking, almost two thousand miles from Lhassa.

For Tenzin Gyatso, the dilemma was becoming insoluble. On the one hand, he understood the all-too-human logic of those who were fighting for their country and for him—and that they were ready to die to defend what he symbolized to them. And he also knew deep down that nothing on earth, not even his own admonitions, could stop this momentum of sacrifice, once it had been set in motion.

On the other hand, he also saw the futility of armed struggle against an enemy of such superior force and numbers. Although Chinese arms were obsolete in comparison with World War II military technology, they were incomparably superior to those possessed by the Tibetans. For a head of state who was barely twenty-two years old, the responsibility was overwhelming and the quandary insoluble, even for a Dalai Lama.

Thus once again he sought solace, if not practical counsel, in his studies. Intuitively, he knew that time was running out for him. He fixed a date for taking his final religious examinations which would confer his unequivocal spiritual authority. A year and a half later, in the spring of 1959, he submitted to examinations and questions from his elders and peers from the monasteries known as the Three Pillars, immediately following the festival of the Tibetan new year.

For the Dalai Lama, these months and weeks were some of the longest of his life. The double game which he was forced to play weighed upon him, and the arrogance of the Chinese emissaries from Peking confirmed his fears about their treachery regarding his country, himself, and foreign relations. He was well aware that they were lying to him and that their underlings were inflicting the most atrocious suffering upon his people. No mercy was being shown towards resisters, and in spite of their facade of courtesy, the Chinese generals now came armed when they appeared before him.

Little by little, Tenzin Gyatso was forced to admit that his country was in the process of being annexed, and that his good will could do nothing to alter it. More than once, he dreamed of resigning his office. The only thing that stopped him was the fear that this would only increase the suffering. He still hoped that the promised visit by Nehru would materialize, and soften the attitude of the invader somewhat. But in the end, the Indian prime minister was never to come—the Peking regime declared that they could not assure his safety because of the rebellion, and canceled his invitation.

The Dalai Lama felt alone and powerless before an adversary whom nothing seemed to be able to affect. With rare exceptions the entire outside world remained silent about the Tibetan tragedy. Neither journalistic nor governmental opinion seemed to be interested in the fate of a country and people which seemed to belong more to imagination and myth than to reality. It was a silence so deafening that it became an accessory to the atrocity.

Entire divisions were sent to reinforce the eastern provinces where the rebels were making things most difficult for the Chinese. Estimates of their troop strength at that time were of the order of one hundred-fifty thousand, something totally without precedent in the high steppes of Asia, where Tibet had been since ancient times a kingdom respected and feared by its neighbors. But this time it was the invader who dictated the terms of the game, and the matchless bravery of proud Tibetan horsemen could do nothing to stop the advance of this pitiless human tide.

The Dalai Lama's days became ever more devoted to his preparatory studies in his refuge of Norbulingka, which seemed like a bubble of protection. But he had no illusions about that, even though he kept calmly to his well-established routine. He had by now come to spend most of the year in this summer palace, where he rose at dawn, typically around five o'clock, to meditate and read. Then he devoted several hours to energetic debate on sacred texts with his elders and teachers. His only distractions were ceremonies, ritual offerings, and traditional public audiences.

In the depths of his being, the constant play of the myriads of dancing flames and shadows from the scores of butter candles which filled the shrine rooms where he spent almost all his time, their lights flickering and gleaming upon the multitude of buddhas and other sacred art, were in the end no more than a gently humorous reminder of the illusory nature of the world of form. From the reports of his aides and subjects, he knew that Lhassa and his entire country were changing fast now, and that the fighting was spreading and growing in intensity. He could also track these changes by the growing exasperation which his Chinese visitors no longer bothered to hide. Like the flickering of the candles, these events, too, were an aspect of the Buddha's fundamental teaching of impermanence.

In autumn, the Tibetans launched a frontal assault from Chushi Gangdruk against the large garrison at Tsethang, the third-largest city in the country, barely two days from Lhassa. This so alarmed the Chinese that Commissar-General Tan Kuan-sen demanded that the Dalai Lama order the Tibetan army to fight the rebels. He also used the occasion to express bitter and violent criticism of his two older brothers and the "reactionary clique" who were fomenting this rebellion from abroad, and sending arms to the rebels. A bizarre detail of his demands was that these expatriate troublemakers be deprived of their Tibetan citizenship. To this demand at least, the Dalai Lama could comply with a shrug, knowing that it made not the slightest difference—his brothers and friends were already safely outside of Tibet, and could not be harmed by losing a citizenship which had now become meaningless.

Having no choice but to accept the Chinese refusal to allow Nehru's visit, the Dalai Lama found himself even more bereft of options and alone before those whom he now had to admit were his enemies. Yet he held steadfastly to the Buddhist teaching that the enemy is also a great teacher, who provides a precious opportunity to learn and cultivate the fundamental virtue of patience. Yet the cost in this case was high indeed, as he would soon come to agree. Meanwhile he followed through on his plan, and passed his examinations successfully one after the other. First he went to the Drepung monastery for several days of lively religious and philosophical debate in which he had to hold his own against a number of scholars, and several thousand monks. He performed quite well, and before returning to Norbulingka, he followed the tradition of climbing to the top of the mountain which overlooked the monastic settlement. He admired the splendid panorama there, but he also could not ignore the stockade surrounded by barbed wire which had been built facing the monastery.

Lhassa was now swarming with refugees, and the tension was extreme. When he arrived at Ganden to continue his preliminary exams, some advised him seriously to take advantage of the occasion to denounce the Seventeen Point Agreement and escape to a safe place. But Tenzin Gyatso felt that such a gesture would be interpreted as an open declaration of war, and used as a pretext for even more bloody repression. Winter now arrived in full force, and the sounds of explosions from battles became rare because of the weather. But there was a nervous expectancy in the air, and hatreds continued to ferment.

As the new year approached, the Dalai Lama redoubled his studious exertions in preparation for the final examinations which he would take immediately following the Great Prayer ceremonies. Before resuming his routine at Jokhang, he received as usual General Chang's formal greetings of the season. The latter spoke of a company of Chinese dancers who were scheduled to visit Lhassa, and asked the Dalai Lama if he would like to attend the performance. He added that, since they already possessed the appropriate theatrical decor, the Chinese military headquarters would be the best place to hold this event. Seeing no ulterior motive in this, he accepted the invitation provisionally, but with the reservation that details would have to be confirmed with his aides who were responsible for planning his itinerary following the new year's rituals and after his examinations were over.

This year's Losar and Mönlam festivities reached a level of extravagance and passion never before seen. By the thousands, refugees and pilgrims filled the great plaza in front of the holy sanctuary, and the tiniest streets were also crowded with the contrasting colors of different kinds of clothing, including the ubiquitous wine-colored robes of monks. The people were eagerly awaiting their young sovereign's appearance, and hoped that this would be the occasion for him to now assume his full pastoral powers as protector of a unique people and culture whose existence was now endangered.

But other, more mysterious influences on the destiny of Tibet were making themselves felt. Sometimes the verses of an ancient prophecy would come to haunt the Dalai Lama, casting a strange light upon his daily meditations and reflections. It is attributed to Padmasambhava himself, the Precious Lotus-Born Master of the seventh century, C.E., who was primarily responsible for bringing Buddhism to Tibet:

> When the iron bird flies in the air
> And horses gallop on whcels,
> The people of the Country of Bod
> Will hecome dispersed over the world,
> And the dharma will go to the land of the red man.

More concerned with his final exams than with Chinese dances, he plunged into his studies, which now took priority over everything else. He argued earnestly with the greatest masters available, sparring verbally with skill and verve, avoiding dialectical pitfalls, and holding his own with the most respected scholars. Finally, Tenzin Gyatso proved himself fully worthy of the title of *Geshe,* a Doctor of Buddhist Philosophy, which his teachers formally granted him at the end of the process—and also worthy of his divine aspect of Ocean of Wisdom, to which they bowed deeply afterwards.

Meanwhile, events outside palace and monastery walls were gathering momentum. On March 5, 1959, the Dalai Lama set out with his entourage to return to Norbulingka. The procession was a grand one, scintillating with a thousand flames as it wound its way along the four miles from Jokhang to the summer palace. Dressed in their most beautiful costumes, common people, nomads, nobles, refugees, and officials turned out by the thousands from Lhassa to greet the caravan, as Tibetan soldiers and bodyguards surveyed the surroundings with hawk-like vigilance.

Curiously, in the barracks and garrisons of the other camp, not a single Chinese was to be seen. Normally officers and envoys from Peking took care to make an appearance at such ceremonies, even minor ones, if only to demonstrate their presence. Neither the common people nor Tibetan officials could find any explanation for this sudden absence.

The next two days went by without incident, and the Dalai Lama settled into his residence at Norbulingka, resuming his normal activities, hoping that this peaceful atmosphere might continue. Then a message was delivered to him, requesting that a date be set for his attendance of the famous Chinese dance performance. He suggested the tenthth of March, three days hence.

Then, on March 9, contrary to all protocol, a Chinese messenger came to see the commander of the Dalai Lama's personal bodyguards, with a summons to visit General Fu so as to discuss how the visit next day was to take place. The latter informed the bodyguard commander that for security reasons the Dalai Lama's journey to the performance was to take place in secret, and that he was to leave behind his usual entourage, accompanied only by two or three unarmed guards. The strangeness of this request surprised and worried the Dalai Lama's aides and associates. But after discussion with them, and not wanting to throw oil on the flames, it was decided that it would be best to comply with these conditions. As a further security measure, the Chinese had ordered that all traffic be banned on that day on the bridge across the river near their military headquarters.

In the early morning hours of the tenth of March, the Dalai Lama arose as usual, performing his prayers and meditation. Then he took a little walk in the garden, enjoying the springtime profusion of flowers and greenery. But soon the gentle breeze which flapped the colored fabric of the prayer flags also brought a strange noise to his ears. It began as a vague and indefinable murmur, and finally grew louder, revealing the shouts and cries of a large crowd which had gathered in the courtyard just outside the Park of Jewels.

His servants informed him that the secret had gotten out, and that a huge crowd of alarmed Tibetans, determined to protect him, had massed around Norbulingka so as to prevent him from leaving. They had heard about the Chinese demand that the visit be made in "simplicity," without his usual bodyguard, and would have none of it. They were aware that a meeting of the Tibetan national assembly was being planned to take place in Peking, and that the Dalai Lama had not yet replied to the invitation to attend it. Above all, they knew that several high lamas who were uncooperative with the Chinese had recently been "invited" on various pretexts to Chinese military camps from which they had never returned. Hence their suspicions of evil designs behind this so-called dance performance, and their determination to prevent the Dalai Lama from attending it.

The day dragged on in feverish negotiations with the Chinese, with many comings and goings, discussions with Tibetan ministers, and with leaders spontaneously elected by the crowd. In the background, there was a murmur of anti-Chinese slogans being expressed with more and more explicitness by the crowd, which refused to budge. At the end of the morning a monastic official known to be a pro-Chinese collaborator tried to slip into Norbulingka—recognized by the crowd, he was stoned to death.

As the tension continued to grow, the Dalai Lama knew he had to calm the people, and decided to inform General Chang that he judged the moment inopportune, and regretfully had to request to postpone his attendance of the performance. The decision was announced publicly by loudspeaker, and was greeted with a roar of joy. Yet the people were still mistrustful, and demanded that his attendance be simply canceled.

At midday, the Dalai Lama sent three of his ministers to explain the situation to the Chinese officials. Their vehicles were detained and searched by leaders of the crowd, to be sure that Tenzin Gyatso was not inside. Then a rotating watch was mounted, so as to prevent any attempt to kidnap him. At Chinese headquarters the ministers' explanations were received angrily. The generals did not hide their venom, and indulged in insults and threats. The Tibetan emissaries took these seriously, and returned to Norbulingka to inform the Dalai Lama of the occupiers' wrath.

Everyone was aware of the gravity of this impasse, yet none could find a way out of it. Just beyond the walls of the summer palace, the anger of the crowd had not diminished, and in the city of Lhassa meetings were being organized to protest the Chinese presence. Towards evening, the bodyguard corps made the decision to refuse to obey any further Chinese orders, whereas the Dalai Lama's admonitions to not inflame the situation went largely unheeded.

A little later, General Tan Kuan-sen sent a courteous message to the Dalai Lama, expressing concern about his security, and offering him refuge with the Chinese so as to protect him from the crowd...he replied with equal courtesy that he fully appreciated the general's concern, but that he did not think it necessary to protect him from his own people. Thus three couriers were sent back and forth in these days of crisis, resulting in no change in the positions of either side.

Reinforced by large numbers of refugees, a great part of the population of Lhassa participated in mounting a permanent guard, in effect a human shield around the summer palace of the Dalai Lama. On March 12, the Tibetans in the city also made their feelings known. Gathering by the hundreds at the foot of the Potala near the village of Shol, they performed a gigantic, spontaneous concert of protest, pounding on pots, pans, and kettles in an interminable cacophony which has never been forgotten in collective memory.

Against the wishes of their young sovereign, a logic of confrontation was now gaining ground. The Chinese authorities demanded the dismantling of the barricades that had been set up at the entrance to the city, but the situation remained an impasse, with an air of heavy expectancy in which anything might happen.

During this time the Dalai Lama urgently sought advice from every possible quarter, engaging in several consultations of the state oracle of Nechung. The latter steadfastly maintained that he should remain where he was and continue his dialogue with the Chinese. Feeling compelled to explore every resource, the young leader also performed several verifications by throwing the dice of the *mo,* a traditional Tibetan practice of individual divination. This confirmed the advice of the Nechung oracle. At one moment he had a severe doubt, remembering a cynical remark his secular prime minister had once made: "When they get desperate, the gods tell lies." But he obeyed the counsel of the oracle. In any case, Tenzin Gyatso realized that on the deepest level events were happening according to an inexorable logic of their own, and that he could only strive to limit the damage.

On the morning of March 16, General Tan Kuan-sen's third letter arrived, leaving no more doubt as to the violent intentions of the Chinese. Underlining this was a special word from Ngabo Ngawang Jigme, who candidly demanded to know in exactly which building the Dalai Lama was staying, "so as to assure that he will not be injured." It was obvious that the Chinese command was planning an assault on Norbulingka, with no regard for the bloodbath this would entail. A similar message was received by the ministerial cabinet. The Chinese had made use of the last few days to prepare the attack and bring reinforcements to secure the city of Lhassa.

Yet the Tibetans continued to mass in huge numbers around the summer palace, refusing any retreat. Only days—perhaps only hours?—separated them from catastrophe. A last effort was made to negotiate, pleading with the Chinese commander to renounce the use of arms against a huge crowd of unarmed civilians. In the great monasteries there was also an atmosphere of heavy waiting, with messengers going back and forth to gather and convey news.

During the afternoon, while officials at Norbulingka were trying to make sense out of a formal acknowledgment they had received from the Chinese, two mortar shells landed and exploded in a pond near the southern door of the palace, causing great consternation and confusion. The crowd outside shouted and raged in impotent anger at this.

That night, the Dalai Lama turned once more to the Nechung oracle.

To his great surprise, the message was now imperative and clear: "Flee! Get away from here this very evening!" Then the medium, a young monk in deep trance, seized a pen and paper and wrote in detail a map of the way to go: it led to the Indian border.

Immediately following this, all debate ceased and preparations began in earnest and were rapidly completed. By dawn, everyone had to be out of Norbulingka, with the Dalai Lama and his family far away in safety. Only essential things could be brought along— his official seals, and indispensable documents and personal effects. His ministers, his two teachers, and a few servants were also in the party accompanying him.

The leaders of the crowd outside were informed of the secret, and agreed to help. They mounted a solid escort around the Dalai Lama and his party, with orders to act discreetly and swiftly. The Dalai Lama wrote out a final appeal, directed to all those who were so ready to sacrifice their life to defend his. He urged them not to engage in fighting unless attacked, and then only in order to defend themselves.

As before leaving on every other long voyage, the Dalai Lama made one last visit to the shrine of Mahakala, the powerful divinity known as Master of Time, where monks were already gathered in prayer. No one spoke. He finally arose and placed an offering of a *khata* scarf before the god's likeness, so that he might be granted a safe voyage—and a safe return someday. Then he paused before a book which lay open, reading a few pages, and came upon a verse from the Buddha offering courage and perseverance to his disciples.

Leaving the dimly-lit shrine, he returned to his own room for the last time, where he exchanged his monk's clothes for the disguise of a soldier's uniform. Then he extinguished all the lights, said a blessing upon the place, and placed a rifle upon his right shoulder and folded an ancient *thangka* (a religious painting made of richly embroidered cloth) which had belonged to the second Dalai

Lama, over his left shoulder. He placed his glasses carefully in his uniform pocket, and walked down the stairs to the door.

He paused at the landing for a moment, and visualized his arrival in India and his return to Tibet. Then he stepped down to where two soldiers awaited him. They led him to the doorway in the outside wall, where his bodyguard commander took over. No noise, no words, not a murmur troubled the deep silence and darkness which surrounded them.

A few years ago, the Nechung oracle had enigmatically declared that "The light of the Wish-Fulfilling Jewel will shine one day upon the West." During this night of the sixteenth and seventeenthth of March, 1959, the Dalai Lama, fourteenth of his lineage and not yet twenty-four years old in his present incarnation, keeper of the timeless wisdom and hope of his people, left his palace and his people for exile, threatened by the invaders of his country. He set out to seek advice and help from the outside world, little realizing that one day the world would come to seek advice and help from him.

APPENDIX

Chronological Reference Points
in the Life of the Fourteenth Dalai Lama

5th day of the 5th month of the year of the Wooden Dog (July 6, 1935)
Birth of Lhamo Thondup in the village of Taktser in Amdo province, Tibet.

25th day of the 8th month of the year of the Earth Rabbit (October 8, 1939)
Official arrival of the child *tulku* of the Dalai Lama in Lhassa.

14th day of the 1st month of the year of the Iron Dragon (February 22, 1940)
Official installation of Tenzin Gyatso on the Lion's Throne.

November 17, 1950
The oracle of Nechung commands that Tenzin Gyatso, though not yet of age, be given full temporal authority over his country.

May 23, 1951
Signing of the Seventeen Point Agreement at Peking by Tibetan emissaries, manipulated by fraud and threats from the Chinese authorities.

1954–1955
Voyage of the Dalai Lama to China.

1956–1957
Voyage to India on the occasion of his pilgrimage marking the 2,500th anniversary of the birth of Gautama Buddha.

February–March 1959
His final theological examinations.

March 10, 1959
Popular uprising against the Chinese at Lhassa, in an effort to protect the Dalai Lama.

March 17, 1959
Flight and exile.

1960
Establishment of his residence at Dharamsala.

1963
The Moscow-Peking schism.

1964
Death of Nehru.

September 1, 1965
Official creation of the Autonomous Region of Tibet, as defined by the People's Republic of China.

1967
Voyage to Japan and Thailand.

1972
Meeting between Nixon and Mao, marking the beginning of full diplomatic relations between China and the West.

1973
The Dalai Lama's first voyage to Europe (Rome, London, Switzerland).

1976
Death of Mao.

1979
The Dalai Lama's first visit to Mongolia; his first visit to the United States.

1980
Hu Yaobang in Tibet.

1982
First voyage to France; first voyage to the Soviet Union.

1986
International ecumenical conference of world religions at Assisi, Italy.

1988
Strasbourg peace plan for Tibet, proposed before the European parliament.

1989–1990–1991
Recurrent outbreaks of violent repression in Lhassa.

1989
Nobel Peace Prize; bloody repression at Tienanmen Square in Peking; fall of the Berlin Wall.

1995
Dispute between Tibetans and Chinese as to the authentic reincarnation of the Panchen Lama.

1997
Death of Deng Xiao Peng. Visit by the Dalai Lama to Taiwan.

1997–2000
A number of voyages to various countries, notably to the U.S. and Europe, in spite of the systematic protests of Peking.

October, 2000
Fiftieth anniversary celebration of the official enthronement of Tenzin Gyatso.

May 23, 2001
Meeting with President George W. Bush at the White House.

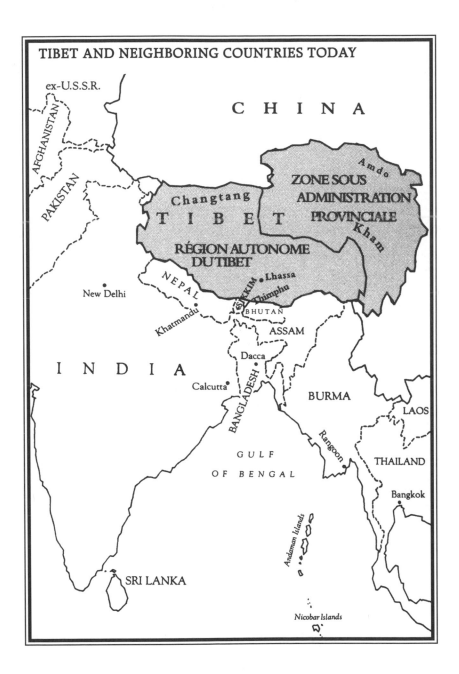

TIBET AND NEIGHBORING COUNTRIES TODAY

Source: Tenzin Gyatso, fourteenth Dalai Lama, *Mon pays et mon peuple, Mémoires* (Geneva: Olizane Publications, 1984).

A Brief Tibetan Chronology

5000 B.C.E.
Pottery and bone fragments found in the Chamdo region.

416 B.C.E.
King Nyatri Tsenpo founds the Yarlung Valley dynasty, and builds the Yambulhakang, the first Tibetan fortress.

620–649 C.E.
Reign of Songtsen Gampo, unifier of Tibet. Creation and development of Tibetan alphabet.

755–797
Reign of emperor Trisong Detsen. The Tibetan empire now extends from the Pamir to Turkestan and Nepal.

Arrival in Tibet of Padmasambhava (Guru Rinpoche) from Odiyan, a tantric Buddhist center in northwest India near Afghanistan. He established Buddhism deeply and decisively in Tibet during his residence there.

791
First monastery built at Samye.

821
First peace treaty between Tibet and China.

11th century
Second expansion of Buddhism. Construction of several great monasteries. Decline of the imperial lineage.

1207
Tibet under the Mongol empire of Genghis Khan, which includes China and most of Asia, from Korea to the Mediterranean, reaching parts of Europe.

1350
Tibet throws off the Mongol yoke and regains its independence. Chinese invasion by the Ming dynasty in 1368.

1357–1419
The great reformer Tsong-Khapa founds the Gelug (Yellow Hat) school of Tibetan Buddhism. Monasteries built in Ganden, Sera, and Drepung (the Three Pillars of Tibet).

1543–1588
Sonam Gyatso, abbot of Drepung, third incarnation of Gedun Truppa (disciple of Tsong-Khapa). He is given the title of Dalai Lama by the Mongol prince Altan Khan in 1578.

1652

Visit of the fifth Dalai Lama to Peking at the invitation of Shun Chih, first emperor of the Ch'ing (Manchu) dynasty (1644–1911).

1720

The Manchu army enters Lhassa, chasing out the Mongol occupiers. The Manchus reorganize the Tibetan government and impose a form of imperial supervision.

1723–1735

Reign of the emperor Kangxi, who withdraws almost all Chinese soldiers from Lhassa. From 1728 on, two *ambans* (Chinese emissaries) represent the Manchu emperor at Lhassa.

1788

Nepal invades Tibet. The emperor Chianlong sends an army to help the Tibetans. Peace treaty signed in 1792. The Tibetan government loses some of its independence to the Chinese, with important decisions now having to be made after consulting the *ambans*.

1795

Death of the emperor Chianlong and decline of the Ch'ing dynasty. Tibet regains its freedom.

1854

Second invasion of Tibet by Nepal, but this time the Manchu forces do not intervene. Peace treaty between Tibet and Nepal signed in 1856.

1910

For the first time, a Chinese-Manchurian army enters Tibet without invitation. It withdraws in 1911, after the fall of the Ch'ing dynasty.

1911

Proclamation of the Republic of China.

1912

The Tibetan government expels all Chinese.

1913

The thirteenth Dalai Lama and the Tibetan national assembly proclaim Tibet as an independent country. Peking refuses to recognize it.

1914

The Simla Agreement. London recognizes the "suzerainty" of China over Tibet, but not its "sovereignty" over it. Tibet is divided into Inner and Outer Tibet. China agrees not to interfere in outer Tibet. But the Chinese government never ratifies the treaty.

1942

Lhassa creates an Office of Foreign Affairs.

October 1, 1949

Mao Tse-tung proclaims the People's Republic of China.

October 7, 1950

Eighty thousand soldiers from communist China invade Tibet.

May 23, 1951

Signature of the Seventeen Point Agreement in Peking, beginning Tibet's integration into China. The treaty obliges China to respect a major autonomy for Tibet.

October 16, 1951
The Chinese army enters Lhassa.

March 10–17, 1959
Popular uprising against the Chinese, followed by bloody repression. The Dalai Lama is forced to flee into exile. Thousands of Tibetans arrested.

September 9, 1965
Proclamation of the Autonomous Region of Tibet. Half of historical Tibet has already been annexed into neighboring Chinese provinces.

August, 1966
The Cultural Revolution arrives in Lhassa. Temples and monasteries still functioning are pillaged or destroyed. Thousands of Tibetans, monks and laymen, are persecuted and sent to labor camps.

September 9, 1976
Death of Mao Tse-tung.

December, 1978
Third plenary session of the Central Committee of the Chinese Communist Party. A reversal of hard-line ideology gains the day. A minimal tolerance of Tibetan religion is instituted.

January, 1979
First delegation of the Dalai Lama sent to visit China and Tibet. Three others follow, but no real dialogue is established with Peking.

October 1, 1987
Demonstrations at Lhassa, with violent repression. Chinese claim six dead and hundreds wounded; independent estimates claim at least the double of this.

March 5, 1988
Renewed brutal repression in Lhassa, with several deaths and hundreds wounded and arrested.

December 10, 1988
Police fire on demonstrators in Lhassa, killing twelve people and wounding many others.

March 5, 1989
Major protests break out in Lhassa, with several days of demonstrations. Martial law proclaimed two days later, with bloody repression. Several hundred Tibetans killed. Martial law remains in effect until May, 1990.

June 4, 1989
Massacre at Tienanmen Square in Peking. Official Chinese estimates are 300 dead; other sources claim as many as 3,000.

October 12, 1989
First meeting in Paris between representative of the Dalai Lama and Chinese dissidents (Federation for Democracy in China).

November 10, 1989
The Nobel Peace Prize is awarded to the fourteenth Dalai Lama.

May 23, 1991
The U.S. Congress declares Tibet to be an "occupied country."

August 23, 1991
For the first time in twenty-five years, a United Nations subcommittee passes a resolution in favor of human rights in Tibet.

1992
Peking declares Tibet a "special economic zone."

November, 1992

The Permanent Tribunal for Peoples holds a special session at Strasbourg devoted to Tibet.

January, 1993

Meetings in London of an international conference of jurists on Tibet.

May, 1993

First meeting between President Clinton and the Dalai Lama.

1997

Official visit of the Dalai Lama to Taiwan. A second meeting with President Clinton. The U.S. government institutes a special coordinator for Tibet.

1998–2000

Chinese set up a "patriotic re-education" campaign in Tibetan monasteries. Hardening of repression. Lhassa now largely unrecognizable because of Chinese destruction and reconstruction. Photos of the Dalai Lama declared illegal.

January, 2000

Escape into exile of the young Karmapa, the third most important dignitary in Tibetan Buddhism. Chinese authorities extremely vexed by this, since this *tulku* had been acknowledged both by the Dalai Lama and by Peking.

July, 2000

Resolution of the European Union engaging its member countries to formally recognize the Tibetan government in exile, if within three years the Chinese still refuse to engage in honest dialogue with the Dalai Lama on the future of Tibet.

April, 2001

An effort at the United Nations to discuss human rights violations in Tibet is thwarted by Chinese threats and manipulations.

The Testament
of the Thirteenth Dalai Lama

March, 1933

As you all know, it was unnecessary to have recourse to the emperor's golden urn in order to verify my reincarnation. The prophecies which had been made by the oracles and lamas, together with the tests I was subjected to as a child, were sufficiently convincing. Thus when I was very young I was recognized and enthroned as the authentic reincarnation of the previous Dalai Lamas.

In accordance with tradition, my education was directed by several spiritual masters, including the regent Tatsak Rinpoche, and Tongdzin Purchokpa Dorjechang. Fortified by their counsel, I plunged into an arduous and thorough study of the essence of Buddhism, from the simplest prayers to the most obscure subjects. They ordained me as a novice and taught me the five foundations of Buddhist philosophy: the *Prajna-Paramita;* the *Madhyamika;* the *Pramana;* the *Abidharma;* and the *Vinaya.* I learned to debate the essential themes of these teachings, which revealed their intrinsic meaning to me. My studies also dealt with the vast sea of affiliations of sutras and tantras, and these marvelous masters gave me many instructions, initiations, direct transmissions, and secret oral teachings. I was constantly and relentlessly immersed in this universe of spiritual tradition day after day, year after year, until my mind was completely saturated with it.

At the age of eighteen, although not yet an adult, I was called to take on the heavy burden of the political and spiritual affairs of my country. I did not consider myself qualified for this job. But my religious and political mentors were unanimous in urging me to accept it, as did the Chinese emperor also and I realized that I had no choice but to do so.

From that time on, I had to sacrifice my personal interests and individual liberty so as to work day and night for the spiritual, social, and political well-being of my country. This responsibility was in no sense a reward, and weighed heavily upon my shoulders.

During the year of the Wood Dragon (1905), British troops gathered around our borders and began to threaten us. The easiest thing would have been to give in to their demands, but such an act would have endangered our independence and our sovereignty. Also, in spite of the difficulty and danger of the trip, I left for Mongolia and Manchu China, two countries with which the "Great Fifth" Dalai Lama had established a relationship of spiritual advisor, reciprocated by their protection, and with whom Tibet had previously enjoyed a relationship founded on mutual respect and support.

A warm welcome awaited me at Peking, where I was received with great pomp by the emperor and empress. They expressed much sympathy when I informed them of the current situation.

It happened that they both passed away during my stay in Peking. The new emperor Chuan Tong succeeded them, and after meeting with him, I set off on my return voyage to Tibet. While I was still on the road, the Chinese *amban* (envoy) in Lhassa concocted some false reports to the emperor, which resulted in a Chinese military force under Lui Chan being sent to invade our country from the east.

Once again, as head of state, I was forced to leave my native country and struggle to uphold our national interests. Despite the rigors of the trip, I arrived with my ministers and high officials in the sacred land of India, where we received refuge. I appealed to the British government to intervene in negotiations with China.

The British made every effort to do so, but the Chinese had now become impervious.

In such circumstances, all one can really do is to pray that things will work out. And our prayers were soon answered, for the power of truth is great, and the forces of karma are certain. A civil war broke out in China, and the situation in Tibet changed completely. Chinese troops stationed there were cut off from supplies, and stagnated like a pond cut off from the current which feeds it. Little by little, we succeeded in dislodging them and pushing them out of our country.

It was in the year of the Water Bull (1913) that we regained control of our country. Since then we have governed ourselves without the least foreign interference. It has been an era of peace and prosperity, in which the Tibetan people have been able to live in joy and harmony.

Many documents of these events exist, and surely you are all familiar with them. Therefore I will not discuss these in detail, only mentioning them so that you know how I read these events. During all this time, I have done my best to preserve our spiritual, cultural, and political identity, and I will be satisfied if my efforts have not been in vain. But I am not speaking of this so that you will thank me—the only reward I hope for is that my country remain strong and my people happy. I desire nothing else.

Now I am getting old, and would like to disengage from my religious and secular responsibilities, so as to devote the remainder of my life to meditation and to my future life. This is something we should all give attention to when our years are advancing.

Unfortunately, it now appears that this is a luxury which is to be denied me. I dare not betray the trust which my meditative divinities and the protectors of the dharma have placed in me. And when I asked my spiritual teachers to give their blessing to my decision of renunciation, they requested that I abandon this and remain in office. In addition to this, the majority of Tibetans seem to have confidence only in myself at this time, and have expressed their strong desire that I change my mind and remain as head of the government. Thus I have no choice but to continue.

This being said, I will soon be fifty-eight years old, and in a short time will no longer be able to serve you. Everyone must realize this and begin to imagine the day when I am no longer there. Between me and my new incarnation, there will be a period of no sovereign.

Our two most powerful neighbors are India and China, and both possess mighty armies. Hence we must establish stable relations with each of them. There are also some smaller nations which maintain a significant military presence near our borders. Therefore, it is important that we also maintain an effective army, made up of young and well-trained soldiers, capable of assuring the security of our country. The five great corruptions now totally dominate life on earth, to the point that war and conflict have become inherent in the very structure of human society. If we do not plan and protect ourselves against this explosion of violence, we will have little chance of survival.

We must especially beware of the barbarous communists, who are sowing terror and destruction wherever they go. These are the worst. They have already spread fire and blood over a large part of Mongolia, and have forbidden lamas there to search for the reincarnation of Jetsün Dampa, the spiritual leader of that country. They have looted and demolished the monasteries, and conscripted monks into the army, killing them on the spot if they refused. They stamp out religion wherever they find it, and even the name of the Buddhadharma has not survived their passage. I am sure you are familiar with the reports that have come in from Urga (Ulan-Bator) and elsewhere.

When the moment comes, we must be prepared to defend ourselves. Otherwise, our spiritual and cultural traditions will be drowned forever. The names of the Dalai Lamas and the Panchen Lamas will be doomed to oblivion, as will those of the pillars of the faith and their glorious reincarnations. Monasteries will be sacked

and reduced to ashes, monks and nuns hunted down and extermi-
nated. The works of our great religious leaders will be lost forever,
and all our cultural and spiritual institutions will be persecuted, abol-
ished, or relegated to oblivion. The people will be deprived of their
rights and possessions, and we will become the slaves of our invaders,
with no option but to wander in vain like vagabonds. All living beings
will be forced to become familiar with human misery. Time will go
by slowly, filled with suffering and unimaginable terror.

Consequently, we must make use of this time of peace and happiness while we still have it, and are able to act freely. We must do
everything possible to prepare and protect ourselves from this coming disaster. We must use peaceful means whenever they are appropriate. But when this is not possible, we must not hesitate to have
recourse to energetic means. Let us work assiduously while we still
have time, so that we do not regret it later.

The future of our country is in your hands. Whether you are a
minister or a minor official, a monk or a secular person, a master
or a disciple, a leader or an ordinary citizen, I strongly urge you to
come together and work for the common good, according to your
abilities. Acting individually, we have no chance of escaping the danger which is threatening us. Forget your rivalries and special interests, and do not lose sight of the essential.

We must struggle together for the good of all, while following
the teachings of the Buddha. If we act in this way, there is no doubt
that with the blessing of our goddess-protector Nechung, delegated
by the Acharya himself (Padmasambhava) to help the Dalai Lamas
in their role as defenders of Tibet, we will prevail.

As for me, I will do everything in my power towards the common
good, and I offer my blessing to those who do likewise. I pray for
their efforts to be crowned with success.

As for those who decline to act appropriately in this critical
moment, their destiny will be their teacher. Although their complacent behavior may bring them momentary benefits, the will

sooner or later be faced with disaster. Now they take great pleasure in watching time go by. Later, they will come to regret their disregard. But it will be too late to change things.

I know that harmony and prosperity will continue to prevail in Tibet as long as I live. But afterward there will be great suffering, and people will experience the consequences of their actions as I have been describing.

My personal experience and my reason tell me that these things will come to pass, and that it is necessary for me to tell you.

A number of rituals have been performed so that I may have a longer life. But the most important thing that anyone can do for me is to take account of this advice. If mistakes have been made in the past, we must learn their lessons. We must work with no reserve, giving the very best of which we are capable.

I will continue to do everything to raise the quality of our spiritual and cultural traditions, and to devote all my energy towards assuring the political stability of Tibet. I encourage all those who have power to do the same, and I pray for them. If we work relentlessly, our people will know peace and joy, and our country will have a long life.

You have asked me for my advice. Now you have it. I beg you to take it to heart and push yourselves to put its essence into practice in everything you undertake. Do not forget what I have said: the future is in your hands. It is extremely important to overcome what must be overcome and to accomplish what must be accomplished. Do not confuse the two.

Translated from the Tibetan by Glenn H. Mullin

Selected English and French Bibliography

Books in English

The Dalai Lama. *My Land and My People*. New York: Warner Books, 1997.
   Required reading for anyone seriously interested in the Dalai Lama and in Tibet.

Mullin, Glenn H., with Shepherd, Valerie. *The Fourteen Dalai Lamas, a Sacred Legacy of Reincarnation*. Santa Fe: Clear Light Books, 2001.
   Highly acclaimed recent book on the lineage, by a noted translator and scholar of Tibetan literature.

Norbu, Thubten Jigme, and Turnbull, Colin. *Tibet, its History, Religion and People*. New York: Penguin 1969.
   By the Dalai Lama's older brother, in collaboration with an eminent anthropologist. A very clear and revealing picture of Tibetan life before the invasion.

Richardson, H. *Tibet and its History*. London: Oxford University Press, 1962.
   A scholarly and thoroughly documented history of the Roof of the World.

Shakabpa, T.W.D. *Tibet: A Political History*. New Haven: Yale University Press, 1967 (reprinted by Potala, New York, 1984).
   The first historical study of Tibet by a Tibetan. The author is the former finance minister, and offers special insights into the political issues of the era.

Stein, R.A. *Tibetan Civilization*. London: Faber and Faber, 1972.
   A classic. Indispensable as an introduction to the world of Tibet.

Van Walt Praag, M. *The Status of Tibet*. London: Wisdom Publications, 1987.
   The most thorough historical study of the legal status of Tibet, and its extremely complex relations with China.

Books in French

Bacot, J. *Le Tibet révolté*. Paris: Peuples du Monde, 1988.
Insights into the fascination of the West with the Land of Snows, and a very interesting Tibetan point of view about life in France during that period (first edition 1912).

Gyatso, Tenzin *Mon pays et mon peuple*. Geneva: Olizane, 1984.
The original version of the autobiography of the Dalai Lama (first edition 1962) in its French translation.

Donnet, P.A. *Tibet, mort ou vif*. Paris: Gallimard, 1992.
The strained relations between China and Tibet.

Collectif. *Tibet, l'envers du décor*. Geneva: Olizane, 1993.
A work which covers diverse aspects of Tibet: historical, cultural, economic, and political, offering a panoramic view of the forces at work behind the scenes.

The Peking point of view

Suyin, Han and Lacamp, Max-Olivier. *Lhassa, étoile-fleur*. Paris: Stock, 1976.
A party-line version, written by intellectuals candid about their fascination with Mao, but willfully blind to the reality of events in Tibet.

❀

About the Author

Formerly a resident of Paris, Claude B. Levenson now lives in Switzerland. She was a scholar of Slavic and Eastern languages, including Sanskrit, before becoming a freelance writer, journalist, and translator. She is the author of a number of other books about Tibet:

Le Chemin de Lhassa (The Road to Lhassa), Lieu Commun, 1985, 1994.

Le Seigneur du Lotus blanc—le dalai lama (The Lord of the White Lotus: the Dalai Lama), Lieu Commun, 1987, Livre de Poche, 1989.

Ainsi parle le dalaï-lama, (Thus Spoke the Dalai Lama) Balland, 1990; Livre de poche, 1993.

L'An prochain à Lhassa, (Next Year in Lhassa) Balland, 1993.

Kaïlash, Joyau des neiges, carnet de route au Tibet, (Kailash, Jewel of the Snows: A Journal on the Road to Tibet) Olizane, 1995.

La Montagne des trois temps, (The Mountain of the Three Epochs) Calmann-Lévy, 1995.

1949–1959: La Chine envahit le Tibet, (1949–1959: The Chinese Invasion of Tibet) part of the collection "La mémoire du siècle" (Memoirs of the Century), Complexe, 1995.

Symboles du bouddhisme tibétain, (Symbols of Tibetan Buddhism) Assouline, 1996.

La Messagère du Tibet, (Messenger from Tibet) novel, Philippe Picquier, 1997.

In collaboration with Jean-Claude Buhrer-Solal: *D'Asie et d'ailleurs, (Asia and Elsewhere)* Balland, 1991.

❀

Books by His Holiness the Dalai Lama and Other Buddhist Titles

Beyond Dogma:
Dialogues and Discourses
By His Holiness the Dalai Lama
$14.95 trade paper, 244 pp.
ISBN: 1-55643-218-6

Beyond Dogma presents a record of a 1993 visit to France by His Holiness the Dalai Lama, recipient of the 1989 Nobel Peace Prize. During a series of public lectures and question-and-answer sessions with political activists, religious leaders, students, scientists, Buddhist practitioners, and interfaith organizations, His Holiness responds to a wide range of topics, including: the practice of Buddhism in the West; non-violence, human rights, and the Tibetan crisis; ecumenical approaches to spirituality; the meeting of Buddhism and science; and more.

Essential Teachings
By His Holiness the Dalai Lama
Introduction by Andrew Harvey
$14.95 trade paper, 152 pp.
ISBN: 1-55643-192-9

"This book is Buddhism purified to its simplest human essence, an essence that transcends all barriers, all colors and creeds. It is a philosophy of the most urgent, practical, active altruism constructed not in a study but lived out at the center of a storm of violence." —from the Introduction by Andrew Harvey, author of *The Return of the Mother* and *The Way of Passion: A Celebration of Rumi*

Blossoms of the Dharma:
Living as a Buddhist Nun
By Thubten Chodron
Foreword by Sylvia Boorstein
$16.95 trade paper, 242 pp.
b&w photos
ISBN: 1-55643-325-5

This book gathers some of the presentations and teachings from a 1996 conference in Dharamsala, India, on "Life as a Western Buddhist Nun." His Holiness the Dalai Lama supported the effort of Buddhist nuns to clarify their purpose in taking vows, widening their context, broadening community beyond their own abbeys, and achieving greater equality with men in liturgical matters, especially ordination.

Buddhist Women on the Edge:
Contemporary Perspectives from
the Western Frontier
Edited by Marianne Dresser
$16.95 trade paper, 338 pp.
ISBN: 1-55643-203-8

Explore this landmark anthology that covers a wide range of issues around gender, race, class, and sexuality in Buddhism. Contributors include Anne Klein, bell hooks, Miranda Shaw, Tsultrim Allione, Shosan Victoria Austin, and others. These essays range across issues of lineage and authority; monastic, lay, and community practice; the teacher-student relationship; psychological perspectives; and the role of emotions.

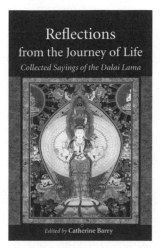

**Reflections from the Journey of Life:
The Collected Sayings of the Dalai Lama**
Edited by Catherine Barry
Translated by Joseph Rowe
$14.95 trade paper, 200 pp.
ISBN: 1-55643-388-3

The Dalai Lama's words of wisdom are collected here from personal conversations with
the author, Catherine Barry, a prominent
television personality in France. The topics
range from violence, death, ethics, and the
environment to desire, happiness, religion,
and humility. The book is divided into eight
chapters and offers contemplations and advice from the highest spiritual authority in Tibetan Buddhism.

**The Tibetan Book of the
Dead for Reading Aloud**
Adapted by Jean-Claude
van Itallie
$20.00 trade paper, 78 pp.
color photos and drawings
ISBN: 1-55643-273-9

Jean-Claude van Itallie's poetic
adaptation of traditional Tibetan
passages to aid and comfort at
the time of death is presented
here, accompanied by vivid pho-
tographs, Tibetan art, and other evocative images. The text leads us
through the stages we experience after death and helps us to overcome
the ambitions, desires, jealousies, and fears that can obscure an understanding of transitions into the next life.